AF478670

# SCENTS OF THE CITY
# 城市的气息
# ODORES DA CIDADE
# ŞEHRİN KOKUSU
# ESENCIA DE CIUDAD
# 都市の香り
# AROMA DER STADT
# АРОМАТ ГОРОДА
# أريج المدينة
# ODEURS DE VILLE

Isabel Naegele
Ruedi Baur

Lars Müller Publishers

## SCENTS OF THE CITY
## Guide to visual stumbling blocks in urban spaces

"Scents of the city" is simply a collection of small samples and patterns from the great variety of public spaces in a city; it is the result of an obsession of many years, an obsession to collect things that, to us, visually denote a "city", the flavour of which is so difficult to describe with words.

All too often the smells and flavours of a city are simple, sad, monotonous or uniform; then again they can be overwhelming like a cheap perfume, and in spite of this—or maybe because of it—they are hardly noticed. But sometimes there will be a surprising freshness, a breeze bearing the merest trace of a scent that captivates our senses and turns everyday banality into poetry. Our ceaseless search for such fleeting impressions changes our perception, and thus those seemingly dull spots, those non-places of a city which normally receive so little attention gradually turn into spaces full of wonder. We decided to call these finds "visual stumbling blocks", a term that attempts to do justice to those banal objects, signs and situations which contribute to the essential character of a city.

These everyday discoveries were collected over a long time and then categorized according to their relationship with each other. By sorting them under certain headings we found it easier to classify them and talk about them. The wide range of cities from which our examples were taken is reflected in the use of different languages. Without claiming completeness, our collection represents a pictorial archive documenting two very different kinds of expeditions through large and small cities of the world. This personal collection was further enlarged by friends who were infected by our obsession and contributed their discoveries. And so this book was born, in which we are trying to put the pieces of the puzzle into some kind of order, capturing a tiny part of those elusive smells and flavours in order to hand them back to the people of the cities and their world.

# 城市的气息
## 城市空间的视觉障碍指南

"城市的气息"只是简单地收集了很多实例，这些实例平时不太引人注意，但它们来自城市生活的方方面面：这是多年来充满激情的视觉上的累积，尽管这确是难以付之言辞的话题 — 对于我们来说"城市"是什么，它的"气息"又是什么。城市的气味和味道通常都是简单、悲哀、单调和始终如一的：但它们又总如廉价香水或附著于舌边令人生厌的味道般顽固、旁若无人。有时，令人精神一振，突然有了一缕清风，这是风的呼吸，夹杂些许香气，让我们的感官为之著迷，也使日常的平庸变得浪漫无比。我们对这稍纵即逝的强烈追求正在改变我们的看法。我们原本毫不在意的城市中的平庸和平凡逐渐演变成充满奇迹和象征的空间。

经过漫长岁月，这些发现形成为一种"城市空间的视觉障碍"概念。这一概念试图公平对待平庸的事物、符号和情形，它们最终进入每个人对城市看法的潜意识中。逐渐地，这些日常的发现被搜集、整理并互相关联。为它们赋予词汇，我们就可更好地谈论它们并给它们分类。城市的多样性和被发现的地方可以用多种语言来表达。尽管我们不会自诩这已经很全面，但我们最终还是有了一个图片集，记录著我们在世界不同城市中两种截然不同的旅行。有同样激情的朋友们也为我们提供了丰富的素材，使我们终于有了这本书。本书试图将许多元素综合在一起，并为整体理出头绪：萃取那些稍纵即逝的气味、芳香和味道，并把这些回馈给城市和属于它们的世界。

# ODORES DA CIDADE
## Guia dos obstáculos visuais em espaços urbanos

«Odores da cidade» é, simplesmente, uma colecção de muitos exemplos e amostras, frequentemente os menos intrusivos, de uma grande variedade de sectores da vida da cidade: o resultado de muitos anos de uma recolha visual apaixonada daquilo que, para nós, constitui uma «cidade» e os seus «odores», por muito difícil que isto seja de pôr em palavras.

Frequentemente, os aromas e paladares da cidade são simples, tristes, monótonos e uniformes; outras vezes, são insistentes e impertinentes, como um mau perfume ou um mau sabor que se agarra tenazmente à língua. Por vezes, felizmente, somos surpreendidos por uma brisa, uma ventarola, que transporta uma réstia de aroma na nossa direcção, que cativa os nossos sentidos e torna em poesia a banalidade de todos os dias. A perseguição apaixonada desses breves momentos altera a nossa percepção. Os locais e não-locais, aparentemente banais, de uma cidade aos quais não costumamos prestar atenção tornam-se, progressivamente, em espaços cheios de maravilhoso e de simbolismo.

Ao longo de um vasto período, estas descobertas foram reunidas sob o conceito de «obstáculos visuais em espaços urbanos». Este conceito tenta fazer justiça aos objectos, aos sinais e às situações banais que, no final de contas, constituem as «entrelinhas» da imagem de uma determinada cidade. Gradualmente, estas descobertas do dia a dia foram recolhidas, listadas e interligadas. Ao lhes atribuirmos palavras, tornamo-nos mais aptos a falar delas e para as classificar. A variedade das localidades e dos lugares descobertos presta-se à utilização de uma grande variedade de línguas. Se bem que não afirmemos tratar-se de uma obra completa, conseguimos, finalmente, alcançar um arquivo de imagens que documenta as nossas duas viagens, tão diferentes, pelas cidades do mundo. Alguns amigos, também entusiasmados, completaram a colecção com as respectivas contribuições, para o livro que hoje temos. Trata-se de uma tentativa de reunir muitos elementos e ordená-los como um todo: extrair esses tão fugazes cheiros, aromas e paladares e devolvê-los às cidades e ao respectivo mundo.

# ŞEHRİN KOKUSU
## Şehir mekanlarındaki görsel engeller için bir rehber

"Şehrin kokusu", şehir hayatının çok çeşitli kesimlerinden, genelde de en az dikkat çeken türden, birçok örnek ve modelden oluşan bir koleksiyondur: Kelimelere dökmek ne kadar zor olsa da, bizim için "şehir" ve onun "kokusunu" neyin oluşturduğuna dair, uzun yıllar boyunca oluşturulmuş tutkulu bir görsel derlemenin sonucudur. Şehrin kokusu ve tatları genellikle basit, hüzünlü, monoton ve tekdüzedir: yani, ucuz bir parfüm veya inatla dilinizden çıkmayan kötü bir lezzet gibi ısrarlı ve küstahtır. Bazen – neyse ki – hislerimizi yakalayıp, günlük hayatın sıradanlığını bir şiire dönüştüren bir meltem, hafif bir esinti, minik bir koku zerresi ile şaşırırız. Böyle anların tutkulu izini sürmek algılarımızı değiştirir. Bir şehirde hemen hemen hiç dikkat etmediğimiz, sıradan görünen yerler, hatta adı sanı olmayan noktalar [böyle durumlarda] ilginçlik ve simgesellikle dolu mekanlara dönüşür.

Uzun bir süre içinde, keşfedilen bu yerler "şehir mekanlarındaki görsel engeller" kavramı altında bir araya getirildi. Bu kavram, sonuç itibariyle, "satır aralarında" bir şehrin bireysel imajına katkıda bulunan sıradan nesneler, işaretler ve durumlara hakkını verme çabasıdır. Yavaş yavaş bu günlük keşifleri topladık, listeledik ve birbiriyle ilişkilendirdik. Onlara sözcükler vererek, onlar hakkında daha rahat konuşabildik ve onları daha iyi sınıflandırabildik. Şehirlerin ve keşfedilen mekanların çeşitliliği, çok çeşitli dil kullanımına uygun düşüyor. Bunun tamamlanmış olduğunu iddia etmemekle birlikte, sonunda dünyanın çeşitli şehirlerine yaptığımız bu tür iki farklı seyahatimizi belgeleyen resimli bir arşiv oluşturmayı başardık. Aynı heves içinde olan arkadaşlarımız, bugün ortaya çıkartmış olduğumuz kitaba katkıda bulunarak koleksiyonu tamamladılar. Bu kitap, birçok unsuru bir araya getirip, bütüne bir düzen kazandırıyor: o anlık koku, aroma ve lezzetleri seçip çıkarıp, onları şehirlere ve onların dünyasına geri veriyor.

## ESENCIA DE CIUDAD
## Guía de elementos visualmente molestos
## del entorno urbano

«Esencia de ciudad» es simplemente una recopilación de numerosos ejemplos y muestras, con frecuencia las menos estridentes, de una gran variedad de aspectos de la vida en la ciudad: es el resultado de muchos años de una apasionada recopilación visual de los elementos que constituyen una «ciudad» para nosotros, y de su «esencia», por muy difícil que sea traducir estos conceptos a palabras.

Con frecuencia los olores y sabores de la ciudad son simples, tristes, monótonos y uniformes: otras veces son penetrantes e impertinentes como el perfume barato o el mal gusto que se aferra tenazmente a la lengua. En ocasiones, por fortuna, nos vemos sorprendidos por una brisa, un soplo de aire, la pequeña sospecha de un aroma que se nos aproxima y cautiva nuestros sentidos, haciendo que nuestras banalidades diarias se conviertan en poesía. La caza apasionada de estos fugaces momentos cambia nuestra percepción. Los lugares aparentemente banales y sin relevancia geográfica de una ciudad, a los que normalmente no prestamos gran atención, se transforman gradualmente en espacios maravillosos llenos de simbolismo.

Durante un largo período de tiempo estas ideas se agrupaban bajo el concepto de «elementos visualmente molestos del entorno urbano». Este concepto trata de hacer justicia a los objetos banales, señales y situaciones que finalmente contribuyen «entre líneas» a la imagen individual de una ciudad. Gradualmente, se han recopilado, listado y relacionado entre sí estos descubrimientos cotidianos. Asignando palabras a los mismos conseguimos poder referirnos mejor a los mismos y clasificarlos. La variedad de ciudades y lugares descubiertos se ajusta al uso de una gran variedad de lenguajes. Aunque no pretendemos que sea definitivo, hemos logrado finalmente crear un archivo de imágenes que documentan nuestros dos viajes tan diferentes por las ciudades del mundo. Nuestros amigos, a los que también ha afectado el virus, han completado la recopilación con sus contribuciones para crear el libro que hoy tenemos en nuestras manos. Se trata de combinar numerosos elementos y dar un orden al conjunto: extrayendo estos tan fugaces olores, aromas y sabores, y devolviéndolos a las ciudades y su mundo.

# 都市の香り
## 都市空間における視覚的つまずきの石へのガイド

　この『都市の香り』は、多種多様な都市生活の実相をさりげなく物語る実例と抽出物の数々を集め、一冊の写真集としてまとめたもので、「都市」の要素とその「香り」といった、言葉として表現することが困難な対象物を、視覚的にとらえようとしてきた長年の情熱の結晶である。都市の匂いや味は、得てして単調で変化に乏しく、物悲しいものであることが多い。そしてまた安っぽい香水の匂いやいつまでも舌先に残って消えないまずい後味のように、しつこかったり気に触るものだったりもする。だが時には、その同じ都市に潜むふとしたそよ風やかすかな香りが、私達の感覚を唐突に呼び覚まし、日常の平凡な風景を瞬間的にポエムへと豹変させることもあるのだ。こうした瞬間を求めて歩きつづけると、私達の視点はおのずと変わってくる。私達が普段ほとんど気にも留めない茫洋とした都会のあちこちが、次第に驚きや象徴性に満ち溢れた場所へと変化していくように思われるのだ。

　長期に渡り、こうした発見は「都市空間における視覚的つまずきの石」というコンセプトに基づいて編纂されていた。このコンセプトは、ひとつの都市に対するイメージ形成の間接的な貢献要因である平凡な物、表徴、場面に正当な評価を与えようとするものだったが、これらの日常的な発見は次第に収集、整理され、互いに関連性を持たされていった。そしてまた、一つ一つに言葉を付記していくことで、より多くが語られ、分類されていった。様々な都市の様々な側面は、やはり様々な言語で語られるにふさわしい。私達の作業はまだまだ終わらない。しかし、世界の都市を巡り歩いた二つの全く異なる旅の記録を、今回は一つの写真集にまとめあげるところまでたどり着いた。同じ情熱に魅了された友人達も、コレクションに貢献してこの写真集を完成させている。こうして作り上げられたこの写真集は、諸要素を寄せ集め、全体に秩序を与える試み —— つまり、ほんのつかの間の匂い、芳香、味を抽出し、それを都市とその独自の世界へと送り返そうという試みの所産である。

## AROMA DER STADT
## Universaler Städteführer visueller Stolpersteine

Das «Aroma der Stadt» ist nichts anderes als eine Sammlung von vielen, oft kleinsten Beispielen und Mustern aus verschiedensten Bereichen des öffentlichen Raums der Stadt; das Ergebnis einer langjährigen visuellen Sammlerleidenschaft nach dem, was für uns «Stadt» ausmacht und dessen «Aroma» sich so wenig in Worte fassen lässt.

Häufig sind der Geruch und Geschmack der Stadt einfach, traurig monoton und uniform; dann wieder aufdringlich und impertinent wie billiges Parfum oder wie ein schlechter Beigeschmack, der sich zäh und klebrig auf unsere Zunge gelegt hat. Manchmal – zum Glück – weht uns aber auch überraschend eine Brise, ein Hauch, eine Ahnung eines Duftes entgegen, der unsere Sinne für sich einnimmt und aus der Banalität des Alltags Poesie werden lässt. Die leidenschaftliche Jagd nach solchen flüchtigen Momenten verändert unsere Wahrnehmung. Die scheinbar banalen Orte und Nicht-Orte der Stadt, denen wir für gewöhnlich wenig Beachtung schenken, verwandeln sich so – peu à peu – in Räume voller Wunder und Zeichen.

Über lange Zeit rangierten diese Funde bei uns unter dem Begriff der «visuellen Stolpersteine der Stadt». Er versucht den banalen Objekten, Zeichen und Situationen gerecht zu werden, die letztlich zum individuellen Bild der Stadt «zwischen den Zeilen» beitragen. Nach und nach wurden diese alltäglichen Funde gesammelt, verzeichnet und in Beziehung gesetzt. Indem wir ihnen Worte zuordneten, konnten wir besser über sie sprechen und sie klassifizieren. Der Verschiedenheit der Städte und Fundorte entspricht die Verwendung verschiedenster Sprachen. Ohne Anspruch auf Vollständigkeit entstand daraus schliesslich ein Bildarchiv, das unsere zwei so unterschiedlichen Streifzüge durch die Städte der Welt dokumentiert. Freunde, angesteckt von unserer Obsession, ergänzten das Sammelsurium durch ihre Beiträge und so entstand das vorliegende Buch. Es versucht die vielen Elemente zusammenzusetzen, dem Ganzen eine Ordnung zu geben und aus den so flüchtigen Gerüchen, Düften und Geschmäcken einen Extrakt herzustellen und den Städtern und ihrer Welt zurückzugeben.

# АРОМАТ ГОРОДА
## Путеводитель по городам среди визуальных ловушек урбанистических пространств

"Аромат города" - это просто собрание многочисленных примеров и образцов, зачастую абсолютно ненавязчивых, извлеченных из огромного разнообразия проявлений городской жизни; это плод многолетнего страстного коллекционирования визуальных символов того, что для нас является "городом" и его "ароматом". Заметим в скобках, что словами это выразить весьма и весьма трудно. Часто запахи и вкусы города просты, печальны, монотонны и однообразны, потом вдруг становятся настойчивыми и наглыми, словно дешевые духи или скверное послевкусие, упрямо липнущее к языку. Иногда - к счастью – нас радует бриз, дыхание ветра, микроскопический намек на аромат, который долетает до нас, захватывает наши чувства и превращает в поэзию банальную повседневность. Увлеченная охота за такими мимолетными мгновениями меняет наше восприятие. Внешне банальные и как бы вообще не существующие для нас места в городе, на которые мы обычно почти не обращаем внимания, постепенно превращаются в пространства, наполненные чудесами и символами.

В течение длительного времени мы объединяли такие находки в единое целое, описываемое концепцией "визуальных ловушек урбанистических пространств". Эта концепция предполагает попытку отдать должное банальным предметам, знакам и ситуациям, которые, в конечном счете, способствуют формированию "между строк" индивидуального образа города. Мы постепенно складывали эти каждодневные открытия в коллекцию, систематизировали их и нащупывали взаимные связи. Мы закрепляли за каждым из них отдельные слова, и это позволяло нам лучше рассказать о них и классифицировать их. Разнообразие городов и открытых нами мест обосновало необходимость использования большого количества разных языков. И хотя мы не претендуем на исчерпывающую полноту нашей работы, нам все-таки в конце концов удалось создать фотоархив, документально отражающий два наших столь разных путешествия по городам мира. Наши друзья, которых «укусила та же муха», дополнили коллекцию своими работами, и в результате получилась книга, которую вы держите в руках. Она представляет собой попытку объединить много разных элементов и сгруппировать их в логичном порядке: извлечь все эти, увы, столь мимолетные запахи, ароматы и вкусы и вернуть их городам и их миру.

# أريج المدينة
## دليل أحجار العثرة المرئية في فضاء الحضر

"*أريج المدينة*" هو ببساطة مجموعة من الأمثلة والعينات الأقل بروزاً في غالب الأحيان، لتشكيلة كبيرة من القطاعات في حياة المدينة: وهو حصيلة سنوات عديدة من العمل الدءوب في جمع صور ما يمثل بالنسبة لنا "مدينة" و"الأريج" الذي تتميز به. إلا أنه من الصعب صياغة ذلك في كلمات. فغالباً ما تكون الروائح والمذاقات التي تميز المدينة بسيطة وحزينة ورتيبة ومتشابهة: وهي أيضاً شديدة الإلحاح وغير ملائمة مثل العطور الرخيصة، أو النكهات السيئة التي تعلق بلزوجة في اللسان. ومن حسن الحظ أننا نفاجأ أحياناً بنسيم معين، أو بهبة هواء، تثير فينا أخف درجات الشك بوجود عبير ما، يتجه نحونا، ويتملك حواسنا، ويجعل من الأمور اليومية المألوفة شعراً.

ملاحقتنا العاطفية لهذه اللحظات سريعة الزوال يغير من إدراكنا. فمن الواضح أن الأماكن المألوفة وغير المحددة من المدينة، والتي عادة ما لا نعيرها اهتماماً كبيراً، تتحول بالتدريج إلى فضاءات مليئة بالأعاجيب والرموز.

وعلى مدى فترة طويلة، ثم تجميع هذه النتائج معاً تحت مفهوم "أحجار العثرة المرئية في فضاء الحضر". ونحاول بهذا المفهوم إنصاف الأشياء والإشارات والمواقف المألوفة التي تسهم في النهاية "فيما بين السطور" في تشكيل صورة متفردة لمدينة بعينها. وتدريجياً، تم تجميع هذه الاكتشافات اليومية، وإدراجها في قوائم، وإيجاد علاقة بين بعضها البعض. وعندما أطلقنا عليها مسميات وصفات، أصبحنا أكثر قدرة على التحدث عنها وتصنيفها. وقد تم توفيق هذه التشكيلة من المدن والأماكن المكتشفة لتلائم استخدام تشكيلة كبيرة من اللغات. ورغم أننا لا ندعي الكمال، إلا أننا توصلنا في النهاية إلى أرشيف من الصور يوثق رحلتينا المختلفتين عبر مدن العالم. وقد أكمل الأصدقاء الذين تملكهم نفس الحماس هذه المجموعة بإسهاماتهم، مما أثمر عن ظهور هذا الكتاب الذي نراه بين يدينا اليوم، والذي نحاول فيه تجميع عناصر كثيرة مع بعضها البعض، ثم ترتيبها ككل: مستخلصين هذه الروائح، وهذا الأريج، وهذه المذاقات، وإعادتها إلى المدن وإلى عالمها.

# ODEURS DE VILLE
## Guide des petites perturbations urbaines

«Odeurs de ville» n'est autre qu'une collection de micro-échantillons relevés progressivement durant de longues années en divers lieux de cet espace urbain contemporain encore public. Senteurs insignifiantes et multiples, souvent tristes et répétitives, se voulant universelles; terribles puanteurs repoussantes que nous nous évertuons pourtant à ignorer; parfum excessif, artificiel, criard, qui essaie de nous interpeller; et parfois, au bonheur, un bouquet charmeur, une effluve éveillant nos sens cachés, un modeste souffle embaumé qui parvient à transformer la banalité en poésie.

À l'affut de telles sensations, notre perception de la ville s'est progressivement transformée. L'espace banalisé souvent non perçu s'est peu à peu métamorphosé en cour de micro-miracles. Longtemps nous avons nommé ces découvertes étranges «petites perturbations urbaines». Leur modestie et leurs capacités à nous éveiller de l'indifférence se voyaient ainsi exprimées. Une à une ces multiples insignifiances qui ensemble créent notre environnement quotidien furent classées, ordonnées, mis en relation. On leur attribuait un nom permettant plus facilement de les retrouver, de les énoncer. Et puisque leurs origines sont diverses, les langues devaient l'exprimer. Progressivement cette collection s'est mise en place sur la base de nos deux parcours à travers cette planète urbaine. Certains échantillons nous ont également été rapportés par des amis chers connaissant notre obsession. Et voilà qu'un objet, le livre, crée la synthèse de cet ensemble. Achèvera-t-il le processus d'accumulation ou ne sera-t-il qu'un relevé d'une situation et d'un temps donnés? Dans tous les cas, il permet de rendre aux citoyens du monde ces odeurs qui leur appartiennent.

# A
## ACHTUNG

**ВНИМАНИЕ**
**ATENÇÃO**
**ATTENTION**
注意
**ATTENTION**
انتبه
**DIKKAT**
**ATENCIÓN**
注意

Achtung
Hühner
ATTENTION
CHIEN BIZARRE

ACHTUNG KINDER
KINDER

Défense absolue
de toucher aux fils électriques
Caténaire sous tension
DANGER DE MORT
MONTECATINI
PERICOLO DI MORTE

Installations de
traction électrique
sous tension
DANGER DE MORT


LEBENSGEFAHR
LEITUNGEN
NICHT
BERÜHREN

红灯停车
灭灯停用

前方道口
小心火车

БЕРЕГИСЬ
АВТОМОБИЛЯ
YAVAŞ

LVB
STOP

Les poux
sont de retour!
Au secours!!
Au secours!!!

# A

## AUTOMÁTICO

**AUTOMATIC**
自动
**AUTOMATIQUE**
**OTOMATIK**
**AUTOMÁTICO**
オートマチック
**AUTOMATISCH**
**АВТОМАТИЧЕСКИЙ**
آلي

DO NOT
ENTER
The Sacramento Bee
Kings sweet parking big downtown tower
The Sacramento Bee
ALL THE BEE
HALF THE PRICE
321-1111
800-284-3733
Singles
NEWS
San Francisco Chronicle
Democratic
Convention

FREE
FREE
For Rent
homes
For Rent
Comic Press
The News in Cartoons
LIC MARKET

by BARBARA
DESPAR
POSTE

LOTTO
TOTO
SPIEL 7
BVG SERVI
U-Bhf Eisenacher S
Bild
KiKi
Petermann
DER FACHGROßHANDEL
KiKi
Petermann
DER FACHGROßHANDEL
LUCK
LIGH
L&M
L&M
enjoyed
in over
60 col

SHERIFF
mini-
Frucht-
Gummi
Wrigley's
chewing gum
EINWURF
TIC·TAC
·citron·orange·
mini-
Frucht-
Gummi
mini-
Frucht-
Gummi
EINWURF
WRIGLEY'S
DOUBLEMINT
CHEWING GUM
23
WENN MÜNZE GEFALLEN,
KNOPF DRÜCKEN
WENN MÜNZEN GEFALLEN,
KNOPF DRÜCKEN
WENN MÜNZEN GEFALLEN,
KNOPF DRÜCKEN
AB Automaten-Braun
RUND·UM·DIE·UHR
AB Automaten-Braun
RUND·UM·DIE·UHR
AB Automaten-Braun
RUND·UM·DIE·UHR

上海地铁
欢迎使用
储值票售卡机
上海地铁
储值票售卡机
自动售卡机

24時間
P
一時預かり
ココ→
月極契約致します
室島上三パーキング
一時預り致します
24時間OK!
一時預り駐車場
P
一時預り致します
泊り1,500円
POKKA
Coffee
SUNTORY
BOSS

# AUTORITAIRE

**OTORITER**
**AUTORITARIO**
権威主義
**AUTORITÄR**
**АВТОРИТАРНЫЙ**
ديكتاتوري
**AUTORITÁRIO**
**AUTHORITARIAN**
独裁

ERTERRASSE

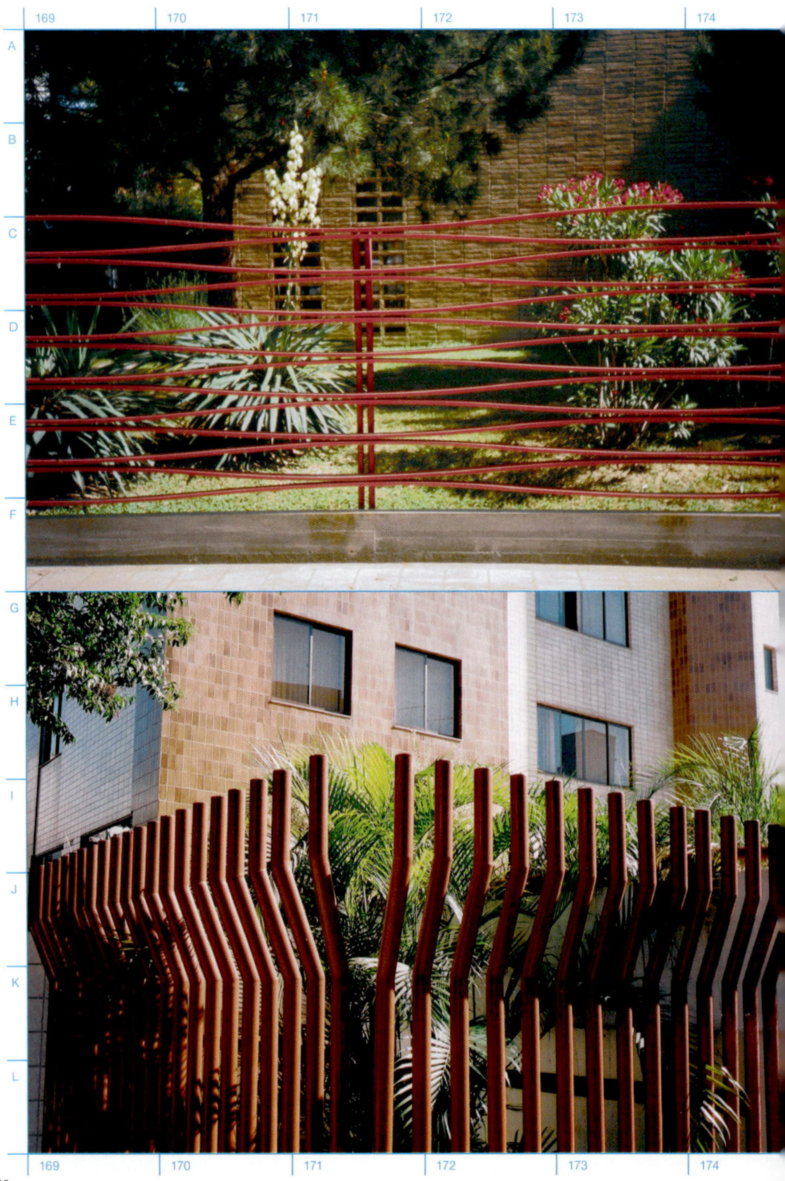

Carrefour

# B

## BEZAUBERND

ПЛЕНИТЕЛЬНЫЙ

بي وتشنج

FASCINANTE

BEWITCHING

迷人

CHARMANT

BÜYÜLEYICI

PRECIOSO

魅惑

# B

**BRANCHÉ**

**DEMET**
**CONECTADO**
束
**VERKABELT**
**ВКЛЮЧЕННЫЙ В ЦЕПЬ**
في حزمة
**LIGADO**
**WIRED**
成捆

C. de la Por
tella.

CARRER
DE LA
PORTELLA

الإسلام
TRESORS
EXPEDITION

# C
## CALIENTE

灼熱
## BRANDHEISS
## ЖГУЧИЙ
ساخن كالفحم
## EM BRASA
## COAL-HOT
炽热
## BRÛLANT
## KOR ATEŞI

Feuerwehr
SIEMENS
Kiss FM

AJUNTAMENT DE PA
COS DE BOMBER
FRESACO
10
50

SPRINKLER
12 TH. FLOOR
STAND PIPE
HIGH ZONE
AUTOMATIC
SPRINKLER
COMBINATION STANDPIPE
LOW ZONE
SPRINKLER SHUT-OFF
4TH BASEMENT PUMP ROOM
HIGH ZONE

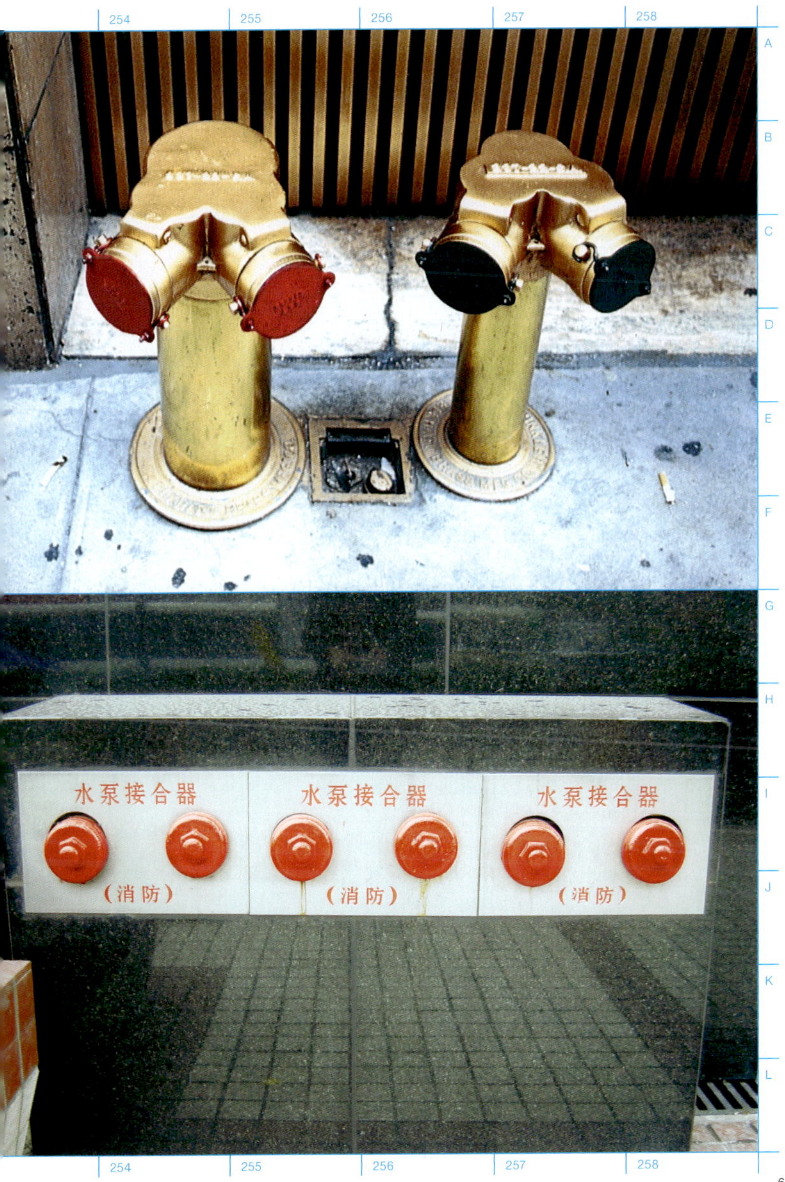

水泵接合器
水泵接合器
水泵接合器
（消防）
（消防）
（消防）

# C
# COMPLEX

复杂
# COMPLEXE
# KOMPLEKS
# COMPLEJO
複雑
# KOMPLEX
# СЛОЖНЫЙ
مركب
# COMPLEXO

СТИЛЬНОЙ
ОДЕЖДЫ
VA
TREND
ОБУВЬ
LORIBLU
VICINI
NANDO MUZI
БИЛАЙН
GSM
СОТОВАЯ
СВЯЗЬ
МТС
GSM
ОФИС
ПРОДАЖ
ВЕЛИРН
МЕХА
КОЖА
ОБУВЬ
LORIBLU
VICINI
NANDO MUZI
ШЕГЕПИСЬ
МОЛОДЕЖНАЯ ОДЕЖДА
Bolero

SA
ORK
30 метров
по переходу
ул.Никольская 5/1
ЮВЕЛИРНЫЙ
$ ОБМЕН
ВАЛЮТЫ
БИ ЛАЙН
СОТОВАЯ
СВЯЗЬ
ОФИС
ПРОДАЖ
МТС
РЕМО
ЮВЕЛИР
ИЗДЕ
Й
МЕХА
КОЖА
ОБМЕН
ВАЛЮТЫ
ПОКУПКА
ПРОДАЖА
ЮВЕЛИРНЫЙ

机
e·STUDIO
TOSHIBA
美丽华办公
用品有限公司
本楼203室
PEPSI
PEPSI
PEPSI
百事可乐
M
甜 品 站

# CONCENTRADO

**CONCENTRATED**
集中
**CONCENTRÉ**
**KONSANTRE**
**CONCENTRADO**
集中
**KONZENTRIERT**
**КОНЦЕНТРИРОВАННЫЙ**
مركز

hr
SKO
Herald Tribune
A.P. MØLLER TAGET I SKATTE-FUSK
POLITIET SKØD ASYL- ANSØGER

Herald Tribune
Herald Tribune
hr
SKO

Pizzeria
Italienische Pizzeria
Andria
Coca-Cola
Pizzeria
Andria
DÜRÜM HOUSE

# C

# CONTRADICTORY

矛盾
# CONTRADICTOIRE
# ZIT
# CONTRADICTORIO
矛盾
# WIDERSPRÜCHLICH
# ПРОТИВОРЕЧИВЫЙ
متناقض
# CONTRADITÓRIO

ADDICT

# CONTRÔLÉ

**KONTROLLU**
**CONTROLADO**
コントロール
**KONTROLLIERT**
**КОНТРОЛИРУЕМЫЙ**
مراقب
**CONTROLADO**
**CONTROLLED**
控制

319
320
321
322
323
324
A
B
C
D
E
F
G
H
I
J
K
L

POLIZEI

POLIZEI

# D

## DECORATIVO

あでやか
**DEKORATIV**
**ДЕКОРАТИВНЫЙ**
مزين
**DECORATIVO**
**DECORATIVE**
装饰
**DÉCORATIF**
**DEKORATIF**

ALDI
MARKT
ALDI
MARKT
ALDI
MARKT
ALDI
MARKT

CATTU

新道商店会

# D
# DESIGNED

СПРОЕКТИРОВАННЫЙ

مصمم

DESENHADO

DESIGNED

设计

CONÇU

TASARLANMIŞ

DISEÑADO

デザイン

# D

# DIRECTIF

# YÖNLENDIREN
# DIRIGIENDO
# 方向づけ
# DIREKTIV
# НАПРАВЛЯЮЩИЙ
# توجيه
# DIRECTIVO
# DIRECTING
# 指導

P
aSTiS
15
M.P.H.

MAMA
Parklaan
P

请在安全线内候车
先下
请在安全线内候车
后上

PECHE
FELIX 8, RUE DU SERGENT BOBILLOT MONTREUIL
P PAYANT
MAPΩNI
Maroni $\frac{\pi}{4} \times 10^3$ m
MARONI PETRA
Retreat
ΑΡΜΟΝΟΚΗΠΟΣ
RESTAURANT
AL VAPORETTO
V-Itinerario
S. MARCO
Brasília
Base Aérea
Terminal de
Cargas
ELEKTRO
WC
KIOSK
Kasse
P
PEDESTRIANS

PIZZERIA
ARSENALE
MUSEO STORICO
NAVALE

PROIBIDO JOGAR LIXO
NESTE LOCAL

## DISCRETO

**DISCREET**
謹慎
**DISCRET**
**SAĞDUYULU**
**DISCRETO**
控えめ
**DISKRET**
**СДЕРЖАННЫЙ**
حكيم

REVOLUTION
GRENZ PUNKT

A 4
BAR TABAC MERCI

Hotel-
Eingang

# E

**ELECTED**

选举
**ÉLECTORAL**
**SEÇILMIŞ**
**ELEGIDO**
選出
**ERWÄHLT**
**ИЗБРАННЫЙ**
منتخب
**ELEITO**

الدائرة رقم
OGNI ELETTORE
OGNI ELETTORE

13
٩٩٦
الاستقــ
شــ
3 2 1
1 2 3
4 5 6
7 8 9
0
BRANCO CORRIGE
Prefeito
Abelardo
PINTO
COLIGAÇÃO
PSDB-PHS
PTB-PST
JEZIEL
23121
45
uma marca pro Aracati
PARA VEREAD
LIDUIN
ESTA SIM É PO
45621 PS

CO
CO
SENSACIONAL
CIRCOCHEN
O SEU VOTO
PODE MUDAR
LISBOA
VOTA
GARCIA
PEREIRA
PCTP
MRPP
www.pctpmrpp.org
RAMILUX

# E

## ÉLECTRIFIÉ

## ELEKTRIKLENMIŞ
## ELECTRIFICADO
## 感電
## ELEKTRIFIZIERT
## ЭЛЕКТРИФИЦИРОВАННЫЙ
## مكهرب
## ELECTRIFICADO
## ELECTRIFIED
## 带电

Pampulha
Conjunto Arquitetônico
Architectural Complex
Conjunto Arquitéctonico

吉大利
如意
方浜中
17
喜铺

# E

## ENCODED

编码

CODIFIÉ

ŞIFRELI

CODIFICADO

暗号

VERSCHLÜSSELT

ЗАШИФРОВАННЫЙ

مشفر

CODIFICADO

B.I.
12
15
9
18

# E

## ENVAHISSANT

## DAVETSIZ
## INVASOR
## でしゃばり
## VERDRÄNGEND
## ВТОРГАЮЩИЙСЯ
## متطفل
## INVASIVO
## INTRUSIVE
## 侵入

CWO
S_D-BER
stil_teknik

530
531
532
533
534
A
B
C
D
E
F
G
H
I
J
K
L
530
531
532
533
534

Nur für Kunden

# E

# EXTROVERTIDO

外交的
# EXTROVERTIERT
# ЭКСТРАВЕРТНЫЙ
منبسط
# EXTROVERTIDO
# EXTROVERTED
外向
# EXTRAVERTI
# DIŞA DÖNÜK

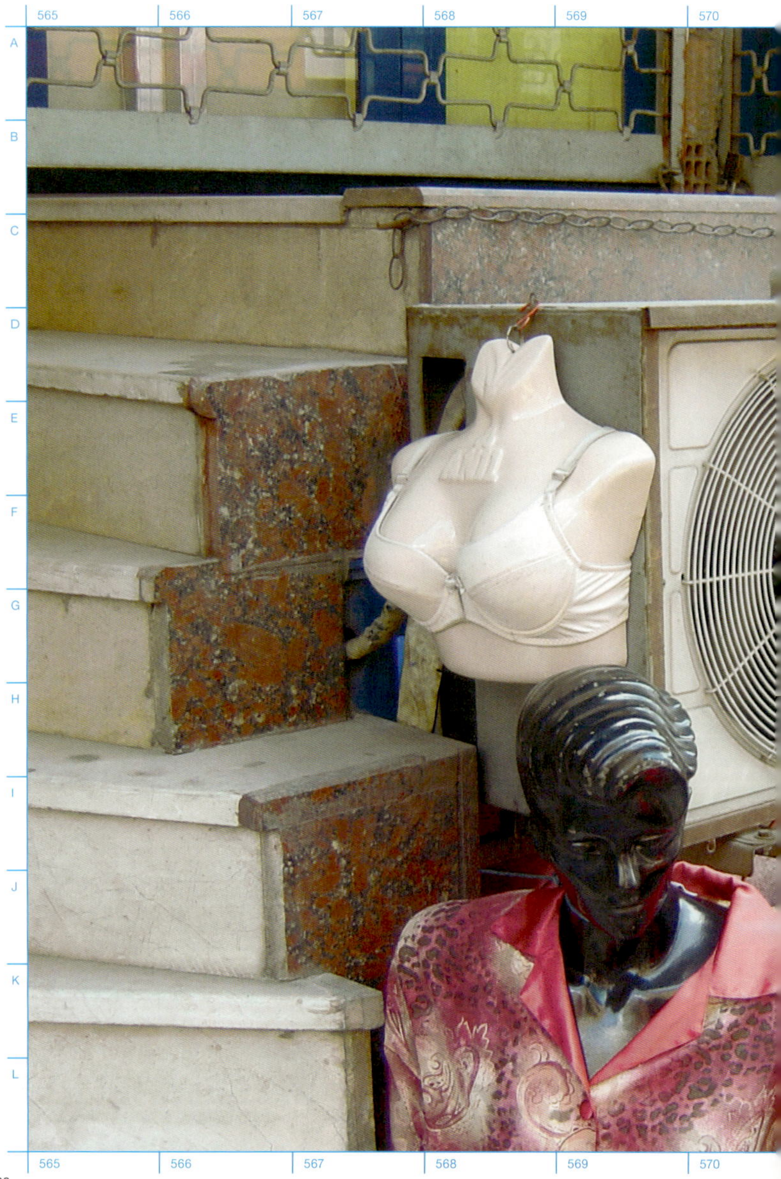

NBB
REFLECTIONS
NBB
LINGERIE

# F

## FEUCHT

ВЛАЖНЫЙ

رطب

HÚMIDO

DAMP

潮湿

HUMIDE

NEMLI

HÚMEDO

湿気

# G

## GEDULDIG

**ТЕРПЕЛИВЫЙ**
صبور
**PACIENTE**
**PATIENT**
耐心
**PATIENT**
**HASTA**
**PACIENTE**
忍耐

LA POSTE

POST OFFICE
ΓΡΑΜΜΑΤΟΚΙΒΩΤΙΘ
LETTER BOX
GR

ΓΡΑΜΜΑΤΟΚΙΒΩΤΙΟ
LETTER BOX
BREV
REGIONALBR
ptt post
郵 便
POST
NO STANDING
AUSTRALIA
POST
Lambik, Sidonia,
Suske en Wiske
zitten nu
op een velletje
postzegels.

# G

## GESCHWÄTZIG

БОЛТЛИВЫЙ

ثرثار

FALADOR

GARRULOUS

喋喋不休

BAVARD

BOŞBOĞAZ

HABLADOR

多弁

643
644
645
646
647
648
A
B
C
D
E
F
G
H
I
J
K
L

工 街
GONG JIE
CNC
TÜRK TELEKOM
telefon

磁卡公用电话
磁卡公用电话
GeKarTel
Hier telefonieren
Sie billiger
OTEL
İŞBANK
TELEPHONE
ČESKÝ TELECOM
ČESKÝ TELECOM

NYNEX
Times Square
42 Street Station
A C E N R S 1 2 3 9 7

中国电信　编号 15536
公用电话

RIKS º STHLMS
TELEFON
RIKS º STHLMS
TELEFON
KS º STHLMS
TELEFON
KS º STHLMS
TELEFON

# G

## GIGANTESCO

**GIGANTIC**
巨大
**GIGANTESQUE**
**DEVASA**
**GIGANTESCO**
巨大
**GIGANTISCH**
**ГИГАНТСКИЙ**
ضخم

CIRCUS CIRCUS
HOTEL·CASINO
FREE CIRCUS ACTS
11 AM TO MIDNIGHT
ROOMS AVAILABLE
If not, we'll place you!
BUFFET INCL BEV $2 69
BRUNCH
DINNER $3 89
BREAKFAST
BUFFET 45 ITEMS
15 HOT ITEMS $2 29
ASSORTED FRUITS
& BREAD S INCL. BEV.
THE STEAK HOUSE
Casual Fine Dining
5pm-Midnite
SKYRISE DINING ROOM
24 HOURS
STATE-OF-THE-ART-TECHNOLOGY
RACE & SPORTS BOOK
PICK SIX PLUS WAGERING
ON ALL MAJOR RACE TRACKS
2ND LEVEL SKYRISE
EASY GARAGE PARKING
PIZZERIA ON THE MEZZANINE
OPEN FOR LUNCH AND DINNER
PINK PONY
24 HOUR
COFFEE SHOP
FULL SERVICE RV PARK

ZOO

rakam
Venny
LOJAS MARIANA
Electrodomésticos
PNEUS BRASIL
JOSEPH
CAD出图
双龙复印社
百兴浴池

Wolford
WIEN PARIS LONDON
Body-
Culture
PHOTO HELMUT NEWTON
WIEN PARIS LONDON

# G

## GLOBAL

全球
GLOBAL
GLOBAL
GLOBAL
グローバル
GLOBAL
ГЛОБАЛЬНЫЙ
عالمي
GLOBAL

Disfrute
Coca-Cola
¡Es Sentir De Verdad!
LA ALCALDI
Disfrute
Coca-Cola
Coke
Disfrute
Coca-Cola
Coke
Disfrute
Coca-Cola
Coke
Disfrute
Coca-Cola
Coke
Disfrute
Coca-Cola
可口可乐

COCA-COLA PRESENTES EN EL
Disfrute Coca-Cola Coke
Coca-Cola

RISTORANTE
Dali
Caffè Espresso
Beba
Coca-Cola
Coke
Enjoy
Coca-Cola
Coke

Beba
Coca-Cola
Beveu
Coca-Cola
Coke
ASIA
ALWAYS
Coca-Cola
Enjoy
Coca-Cola
Coke
- TOYS
PAYPHONE

746
747
748
749
750
Pains à la ligne.
Coca-Cola
Carlsberg
Enjoy
Coca-Cola
Coke
TRADE MARKS REGD.
ΧΟΝΔΡΙΚΕΣ & ΛΙΑΝΙΚΕΣ
ΤΗΛ. 332979-332788
Ανοικτό και Κυριακή
ΠΟΡΙΚΟΝ ΚΕΝΤΡΟΝ ΖΥ
ΡΕΟΠΩΛΕΙΟΝ - ΙΧΘΥΟΠΩΛΕΙΟΝ - ΠΑΝΤΟΠΩ
ΝΤΑ ELENA
Snapple
Enjoy
Coca-Cola
Coke
TRADE MARKS REGD.
ΧΑ
SUPE
Pilsen
BİRA
soğuk içiniz
Coca-Cola
330 ml.

Enjoy
Coca-Cola
ΣΤΙΑΤΟΡΙΟΝ-BAR
ΧΡΥΣΟΣΤΟΜΟΣ
Enjoy
Coca-Cola
ΕΓΧΡΩΜΑ ΚΛΕΙΔΙΑ ★ ΣΦΡΑΓΙΔΕΣ
★ ΔΙΑΦΗΜΙΣΤΙΚΑ
ΔΗΜΗΤΡΙΟΣ ΙΩΑΝΝΟΥ
(ΠΠΟΛΟΣ)
protasi
craft shop
gallery
• Original ceramics
• Selfdesigned jewellery
• Engravings • Rangs
• Dried flowers baskets
200m ahead
IMPORTED
CASUALS
雪碧
Enjoy
Coca-Cola
NEC
maxell

# G

## GRÜN

ЗЕЛЕНЫЙ

أخضر

VERDE

GREEN

绿色

VERT

YEŞIL

VERDE

绿

Wege und Treppen
werden bei Eisglätte
oder
nach Schneefall
nicht abgestreut!
Betreten erfolgt
auf eigene Gefahr.
Magistrat
der Stadt Darmstadt
爱花木
美化心灵
La propreté fleurit!
Es blüht
die Sauberkeit!
Cleanliness reigns supreme!
Fiorisce la pulizia!
رئيس قسم
الاتصالات الإدارية

LÜTFEN
ÇİÇEKLERİ
KOPARMAYIN
مدينة مكناس
بمحافظتنا على النباتات
نحافظ على جمال
مدينتنا
请勿进入草坪
KEEP OFF THE GRASS
青青芳草情
依依游人心

PROIBIDO
PISAR

# H

**HARMONIOSO**

調和
**HARMONISCH**
**ГАРМОНИЧНЫЙ**
ملاءمة
**HARMÓNICO**
**HARMONIZING**
和谐
**HARMONIEUX**
**UYUMLU**

ARASI
SALİH ÖZTÜRK

POSTES
Réservé aux
gens de
passage

# H

**HERMÉTIQUE**

**BÜYÜSEL**
**HERMÉTICO**
密封
**HERMETISCH**
**ГЕРМЕТИЧЕСКИЙ**
سحري
**HERMÉTICO**
**HERMETIC**
封闭

87
Privatgrundstück
88
89

800
801
802
803
804
A
B
C
D
E
F
G
H
I
J
K
L
800
801
802
803
804

PRIVADO
PROHIBIDO APARCAR
SE AVISA A GRÚA

# H

## HIMMLISCH

**АНГЕЛЬСКИЙ**
سماوي
**ANGÉLICO**
**HEAVENLY**
天堂
**DIVIN**
**HARIKA**
**ANGELICAL**
至福

# HUMANO

人
## MENSCHLICH
## ЧЕЛОВЕЧНЫЙ
إنساني
## HUMANO
## HUMAN
人类
## HUMAIN
## İNSAN

依次排队
LINE UP IN PROPER ORDER

HIER NIET

R 85

AVANTI

872
873
874
875
876
A
B
C
D
E
F
G
H
I
J
K
L
872
873
874
875
876

# INSEPARABLE

不可分离
INSÉPARABLE
AYRILMAZ
INSEPARABLE
分離不可
UNZERTRENNLICH
НЕОТДЕЛИМЫЙ
لا يمكن فصله
INSEPARÁVEL

# J

## JEUNE ET JOLIE

## GENÇ VE GÜZEL
## JÓVENES Y GUAPAS
## 若く美しく
## JUNG UND SCHÖN
## МОЛОДЫЕ И КРАСИВЫЕ
## شاب وجميل
## JOVENS E BONITAS
## YOUNG AND PRETTY
## 年轻貌美

DEMRE BELEDİYESİ
ÇEVREMİZİ TEMİZ TUTALIM
LIXO
DUBAI MUNICIPALITY
KEEP IT CLEAN
Ihr Clean-Spatz hält den Bahnhof sauber

果皮箱
果皮箱
不可回收垃圾
NON-RECYCLABLE
cash box
A LOJA DE JEANS
Abfälle
déchets
rifiuti
litter
果皮箱
DUSTBIN

Leergebinde

BAUHAUS

LIXEIRA DE USO
EXCLUSIVO DA
SIDECON

949
950
951
952
953
954
A
B
C
D
E
F
G
H
I
J
K
L
BOUQUET

# K

# KOMMERZIELL

**КОММЕРЧЕСКИЙ**

تجاري

# COMERCIAL
# COMMERCIAL

商业

# COMMERCIAL
# TICARI
# COMERCIAL

商売

Nº 143

5499,-
4295,-
1659,-
5499,
ohne Beschriftung
mit Beschriftung
Anna + Felix

100g
本場素干桜海
北海道
六五〇
七〇〇
香信五
二・八
鰹削パック
味つ勝買
冬菇一〇〇グラム
九五〇
四
LE
mit
Lizenz
SALE
mit
Lizenz
HORARIO
NES A VIERNES
Y DE 16:30 A 20
DO DE 10 A 14 H.
FOTOS
-CARNET-
AL ACTE
para Fotos
Bodas
Comuniones
Bautizos
Nacimientos
para Foto
Solo 3.000 Ptas

# LABORIEUX

ZAHMETLI
LABORIOSO
骨折り
MÜHSAM
ТРУДОЛЮБИВЫЙ
مجد
LABORIOSO
LABORIOUS
艰辛

ÇALIŞMALARI, İIZIN VERMİŞ OLDUĞ
RAHATSIZLIKTAN DOLAYI
SAYIN HALK MIZDAN ÖZÜR DİLERİZ
İRA İNŞAAT
A. MÜFİT GÜRTUNA
İSTANBU BÜYÜKŞEHİR BELEDİYE BAŞKANI

S. KOULENDROS
CONSTRUCTION
TROTTOIR
BARREE
TROTTOIR
BARREE
ACCES
A LA GARE
SNCF Gare Lyon Part Dieu
RUE
BARREE
Déviation Déviation
PASSAGE
INTERDIT
AUX PIETONS
PIETONS
VEUILLEZ
TRAVERSER
PIETONS
SANS ISSUE
VIETATO
L'ACCESSO
AI NON ADDETTI
AI LAVORI

# LECKER

**АППЕТИТНЫЙ**

منمق

**DELICIOSO**

**LUSCIOUS**

甘美

**DÉLICIEUX**

**HOŞ**

**DELICIOSO**

甘美

Self Servic
SEM BALAN
01 PRATO com
01 Pedaço CARN
2,50
GUARAMA'
"COPO"   0,5


DÖNER KEBAB
2,50
nach..
DÖNER
Art


PIZZA MILANO
Şükrü Usta
EVLERE SERVİS YAPILIR. TEL.8122939


Eis Snacks
Fisch
Steaks
Salate
Haus

Gizzi
Spargel
Steinbeisser
Trink Coca-Cola Cola
echt fruchtig-frisch
Libella
SEMİZOTU
KURU
FASULYE
MANTI
PİLAV
ÇORBA
IZGARA
MENEMEN

Gouda's Glorie
de PRINSEKEL
Heden aanbevolen
VERSE GEBAKKEN BROODJES
Uit eigen keuken
vers beleg
Gebakken warm vlees
hip. shoarma
+ Div. soep , salades
en warme maaltijden
KREUZ
Wild
Zeit

Bier Garten
KRAUT u. KRUSTE
GOOD
TRADITIONAL
FOOD
GUTE
BÜRGERLICHE
KÜCHE

Hier esse
und pre

Sie gut
wert

RISTORANTE RIFUGIO G. SAPIENZA
MENU' TURISTICO
PRIMO PIATTO - SECONDO PIATTO
CONTORNO - FRUTTA

# L

# LIMITING

有限
**LIMITATIF**
**SINIRLAYICI**
**RESTRICTIVO**
限定
**EINGRENZEND**
**ОГРАНИЧИВАЮЩИЙ**
محدد
**LIMITATIVO**

1081
1082
1083
1084
1085
1086
A
B
C
D
E
F
G
H
I
J
K
L
1081
1082
1083
1084
1085
1086

1088
1089
1090
1091
1092
A
B
C
D
E
F
G
H
I
J
K
L

# LITTÉRAL

# KELIMESI KELIMESINE
# LITERAL
# 制限
# BUCHSTÄBLICH
# БУКВАЛЬНЫЙ
# حرفي
# LITERAL
# LITERAL
# 平实

DIRECTION: PAUL
JAZZ
VENDREDI 1
GLOBA
NUIT BLAN
RACHID T
UN DA MEN

TE ET PATRICIA COQUA
PRESENTE
C
AVRIL 1996 A 21 H
GROO
A L' OLYMP
HA . SYST
AL . JOSH

gio
PISCIN
CIE
COLON
neutral
mobil
Berdel
inter

CORNOS
58 JJ
59 LOLOLA
60 AU
61 VALMIR
1- ANTC
23 CHOCOLATE
24 MARINHO
25 BRANDÃO
26 MANCO
27 MANINHO
28 ALEX
EVANDRO MESTRE
62 NEGO
63 ALVARO
2-
3- LO
4- PRE
5- ETE
6- ZÉ
DED
AL SENATORE ANTONIO BERNOCC
L COMUNE DI MILANO DEDI
UESTO PALAZZO DELL' A
A LUI DONATO ALLA CI
N IL CONCORSO DEI FRAT
CHELE E ANDREA BERNO
MCMXXXIII

大学生活动中
广大同学学习
实践应用能力
了所有机器的
些应用软件。另
放，管理员热情
课外科技实践活
开放时间：
周一至周五 中

51
DUR

# L

## LÚDICO

遊び好き
VERSPIELT
ИГРИВЫЙ
لعوب
LÚDICO
PLAYFUL
嬉戏
LUDIQUE
NEŞELI

SYSTEM ODEON
RITA
STEM
BARBA DARRA

1153
1154
1155
1156
1157
1158

# M

## MERDIQUE

İĞRENÇ
ASQUEROSO
不愉快
BESCHISSEN
ДЕРЬМОВЫЙ
بائس
MÉRDICO
SHITTY
低劣

HUNDE

R
Peppenhovener
Hunde-Bar

Gassi
Ville de
Montpellier
M
TOUTOUNET
...!
1 ENFILEZ
LE SAC
2 SAISISSEZ
LA DEJECTION
3 RETOURNEZ
LE SAC
CORBEILLE
4 JETEZ
LE SAC
pour prendre le sac
TIREZ
(sacs non alimentaires)
POR UMA FREGUESIA
MAIS LIMPA!
Junta de Freguesia
BRAVO
UHV
Hundebesitzer
NEHMT RÜCKSICHT !
Im Falle eines »Falles « ... für gleich oder später
Tüte ziehen
UHV

BRAVO
BRAVO
Ablage
fond

CHIENS
INTERDITS
Privatgrundstück
Bulgarische Botschaft

楯町児童公園
糞
公園管理課
HIER NIET

MÊME TENUS EN LAISSE

ACHTUNG
HUNDE BITTE AN DIE LEINE!
ATTENZIONE
CANI AL GUINZAGLIO PREGO!
HUNDE AN DIE LEINE
CANI AL GUINZAGLIO
GARTENAMT
HAF
HAF
ACCÈS
INTERDIT AUX CHIENS

an
Markttagen

# M

## MÓVEL

MOBILE
移动
MOBILE
MOBIL
MÓVIL
移動式
MOBIL
МОБИЛЬНЫЙ
متنقل

FECHE O
VIDRO AR
CONDICIONADO
CABRERA
TRANSPORTES
TELF. (91) 6957504-12
FAX (91) 6957697
VAMOS HACIA EL FUTURO... SIGUENOS

ΕΞΟΔΟΣ ΚΛΕΙΣΤΗ
ΠΑΡΑΚΑΛΩ ΧΡΗΣΙΜΟΠΟΙΕΙΣΤΕ
ΑΛΛΗ ΕΞΟΔΟ
EXIT CLOSED
PLEASE USE OTHER EXIT

自転車放置禁止区域
大阪市

1232    1233    1234    1235    1236
A
B
C
D
E
F
G
H
I
J
K
L

OBRE A 15H00
PORTES 1H30 AVANT LE SPECTACLE
with 37 ST. Clear Channel Entertainment  Good News Productions AG and Opus One SA
www.riverdance.com
PHENOMENON
UBS
touring

HAPPY MUSIC
DIESEL
4
3

# N

**NOMMÉ**

**ADI GEÇEN**
**NOMINADO**
指名
**NÄMLICH**
**НАЗВАННЫЙ**
محدد
**NOMEADO**
**NAMED**
命名

Siller - Weg
Nach Sillerwies
Sillerwies
Sankt Annæ Plads
30 - 24
SEMINÁŘSKÁ
STARÉ MĚSTO - PRAHA 1
CAMPBELL LANE
கேம்பல் சந்து
Ruelle des
Ursulines
GOUDEN-HAND-
STRAAT
PONTE
BERNARDO

GREAT SUFFOLK STREET SE1
BANKSIDE
TATE →
SHAKESPEARE'S GLOBE →
SOUTHWARK STREET →
DISCOTHEQUE
1er ARR!
RUE
Giuseppe VERDI
COMPOSITEUR
1813~1901
1er ARR!
PETITE RUE
PIZA
TRAVESSA
DA CONCEIÇÃO
DA GLÓRIA
Via Purtum
11me .ARR!
RUE
JULES
VALLÈS
3
КРАСНАЯ
ПЛОЩАДЬ
东 大儒巷 西
E DARU XIANG W

CALLE
DEL FORNO
2078
RUDE
FANS

# N

# NUMEROUS

众多
# NOMBREUX
# ÇOK
# NUMEROSO
大群
# ZAHLREICH
# МНОГОЧИСЛЕННЫЙ
عديد

# NUMEROSO

1261
1262
1263
1264
1265
1266
589
H1
14 → 17
H1
1 → 8
16
10
10
TRŽIŠTĚ
263
100DEM
1600
100USD
3550
WE BUY
NETTO
P30
25
17
9 9
11
2 RESTE
SEMAINES
2 RESTE
SEMAINES
LAVAGE
7KG
24F
10KG
40F
SECHAGE
Carlton is lowest.
Subway
A AA B CC D 1
振興街 36
Normal
170
3
4
Super
480
380
2
5

23
35
70
4
CASSYPHON
No 13
8m1
m8.5
SCHIEBER
No 70
SCHIEBER
No 71
GIRLS
GIRLS
GIRLS
25¢
LIVE
PRIVATE BOOTHS
103
1
1575
64
Films
10F
8
33
1
SOKKEN
118
149
ANO
1654
IAFA
DSIDO
1-
PER PAR

SU
8/33
Ç.T.V.
0167
Ç.T.V.
0166
550-07
022

# N
## NUTRITIOUS

营养
### NOURRISSANT
### BESLEYICI
### NUTRITIVO
栄養豊富
### NAHRHAFT
### ПИТАТЕЛЬНЫЙ
مغذي
### NUTRITIVO

Cosmo
Cosmo
for
your
hair

مانع الأسنان
DENTISTE
عيادة الأطلس
للبيطرة

ΚΡΕΟΠΩΛΕΙΟΝ

Fleisch
&
Wurst
Mo.-Fr. 8-18.30
Sa. 8-13

# O

OMNIPRÉSENT

HAZIR VE NAZIR
OMNIPRESENTE
偏在
ALLGEGENWÄRTIG
ВЕЗДЕСУЩИЙ
كلي الوجود
OMNIPRESENTE
OMNIPRESENT
无处不在

Abendakademie
Serenadenkonzert
6. Juli 2002, 19 Uhr
Mannheimer
Abendakademie
Serenadenkonzert
6. Juli 2002, 19 Uhr
Mannheimer
Abendakademie
Serenadenkonzert
6. Juli 2002, 19 Uhr

Abendakademie
Serenadenkonzert
6. Juli 2002, 19 Uhr
Eintritt: 8 €
Mannheimer
Abendakademie
Zum 25-jährigen Jubiläum
des Kammerorchesters
der Abendakademie
Serenadenkonzert
6. Juli 2002, 19 Uhr

For your personal safety and
security, video-linked TV
cameras maintain constant
recorded surveillance of
this train. CCTV evidence
can be used in a court of law.
SouthCen
Welcome to LONDO
Dieser Bereich wird zu Ihrer Sicherheit von
der Polizei videoüberwacht.
Aufgrund der begrenzten Aufzeichnungsdauer wenden Sie sich
bei besonderen Vorfällen bitte unverzüglich an die Polizei.
The police is supervising this area by video.
Because of limited recording capacity please inform the police without
delay if you notice extraordinary or suspicious incidents.
Bu mekan sizin emniyetiniz için Polis tarafından
kamera ile gözetlenmekte.
Kamera kayıdı sınırlı oldugundan dolayı hususi vakalarda hemen Polisi arayın.
STADT MANNHEIM
Notruf: 110
Auskunft: 174-0 oder 174-2333

REGGIO EMILIA
AVENUE
MARÉCHAL
DE LATTRE DE TASSIGNY
34

1333
1334
1335
1336
1337
1338
A
B
C
D
E
F
G
H
I
J
K
L
Restaura
SORTIE
1333
1334
1335
1336
1337
1338

deoüberwachung
Bitte lächeln!
EVRE
EKONOMİ
GAZETESİ
HAN KARŞISI HUZUR APT.
KAT 4'E TAŞINMIŞTIR
KURULUŞ YILI 1944
KAT 3
Neue Zürcher Zeitung
ИНДИЙ
КУХН

nald's
麦 当 劳
Gerüst GmbH
GRUNDIG

# O

# ORNAMENTAL

**ORNAMENTAL**
装潢
**ORNEMENTAL**
**SÜSLEYICI**
**ORNAMENTAL**
飾りもの
**ORNAMENTAL**
**ДЕКОРАТИВНЫЙ**
زخرفي

# P

**PLANO**

自然回帰
**BODENSTÄNDIG**
**ПРОСТОЙ**
واقعي
**COMESINHO**
**DOWN-TO-EARTH**
朴实
**TERRE À TERRE**
**AYAĞI YERE BASAN**

KⓇL
2843
MERIT
5827

294

1400
1401
1402
1403
1404
A
B
C
D
E
F
G
H
I
J
K
L
1400
1401
1402
1403
1404

LOOK LEFT
LOOK RIGHT
LOOK LEFT
LOOK RIGHT
LOOK
LOOK
LOOK RIGHT

# P

**PRIVAT**

**ЧАСТНЫЙ**
خاص
**PRIVADO**
**PRIVATE**
隐私
**PRIVÉ**
**ÖZEL**
**PRIVADO**
私的

Wir haben Eure Zerstö-
rungswut der Polizei
gemeldet und sie wird sich
bemühen Euch ausfindig
zu machen !
Privat-Besitz
Durchgang verboten
PROPRIÉTÉ PRIVEÉ
PASSAGE INTERDIT

# P

# PROTECTED

保护
# PROTÉGÉ
# KORUMALI
# PROTEGIDO
保護
# BESCHÜTZT
# ЗАЩИЩЕННЫЙ
محمي
# PROTEGIDO

Tessuti
Tessuti

RESTAURANTE
PONTOFRIO
City & Street
Equipamentos Urbanos
Carrefour
PAMPULHA
SUPERMERCADO
BARRIGA CHEIA
225-2696
BELO HORIZONTE
BEL LAR
ACABAMENTOS
ESTACIONE AQUI
BELO HORIZONTE

1448
1449
1450
1451
1452

NO
PARKING
VIOLATORS
WILL BE
TOWED AWAY
AT OWNERS
EXPENSE

# P

**PROTESTATAIRE**

**PROTESTO**
**PROTESTANDO**
抗議
**PROTESTIEREND**
**ПРОТЕСТУЮЩИЙ**
احتجاجي
**CONTESTATÁRIO**
**PROTESTING**
抗议

MAJORCA
IST NICHT
HIER
MAJORCA
IST NICHT
HIER

POGO1
MYHOS
MAJORCA
IST NICHT
HIER
IST NICHT
HIER

ATUREM
LA GUERRA!
MON AME
D'ARTISTE A
LE MEME
SEXE

Spitalgasse
44
Je suis BUSHBÉE DEVANT
TA CONNERIE
EMRET CONI! EMRET CON

Amour

# P

# PROVISIONAL

即興
## PROVISORISCH
## ВРЕМЕННЫЙ
ارتجالي
## IMPROVISADO
## IMPROVISED
即兴
## PROVISOIRE
## DOĞAÇLAMA

İSTANBUL KUYUMCULAR ODASI
YAKINDA KENDİ BİNASINDA
HİZMETİNİZDEDİR
ÇEVREYE VERDİĞİMİZ RAHATSIZLIKTAN
DOLAYI ÖZÜR DİLERİZ
İSTANBUL KUYUMCULAR ODASI

# P

## PUBLIC

**HALK**
**PÚBLICO**
公的
**ÖFFENTLICH**
**ПУБЛИЧНЫЙ**
عام
**PÚBLICO**
**PUBLIC**
公共

MINISTÈRE DE L'ÉCONOMIE ET DES FINANCES
Nationale d'Interventions Domaniales, 17, rue Scribe, 75009 Paris
E AUX ENCHÈRES PUBLIQUES
à l'extinction des feux
JEUDI 27 JUIN 1996 à 14 h
à VERSAILLES
re des Yvelines, place André Mignot, Salle Palewski
TERRAINS
LIBRES sauf les lots 1, 9 et 16 (occupés sans titre)
CONDITIONS PRINCIPALES DE LA VENTE

MINISTÈRE DE L'ÉCONOMIE ET DES FINANCES
Direction Nationale d'Interventions Domaniales, 17, rue Scribe, 75009 Paris
VENTE AUX ENCHÈRES PUBLIQUES
à l'extinction des feux
MERCREDI 19 JUIN 1996 à 13 h
à PARIS 9e
Salle des Ventes, D.N.I.D., 17, rue Scribe
APPARTEMENTS - CHAMBRES
LIBRES sauf les lots VII (occupé) et VIII (occupé sans titre)
CONDITIONS PRINCIPALES DE LA VENTE

à PARIS (19ème)
7 bis, rue Bellot
UN STUDIO
au 3me étage
et UNE CAVE
MISE A PRIX ( ) 30.000 F
UN APPARTEMENT
au troisième étage,
DE DEUX PIECES PRINCIPALES
CAVE
à PARIS (14ème)
62, rue Didot
L'ADJUDICATION AURA LIEU LE
JEUDI 19 DECEMBRE 1996 à 14 H 30
MISE A PRIX : 150.000 F

EN UN LOT
UN APPARTEMENT
de 4 PIECES PRINCIPALES
et UNE CAVE
à CRETEIL (94)
2-12, rue Camille Dartois
MISE A PRIX ( ) 200.000 F
VENTE SUR LIQUIDATION JUDICIAIRE
EN UN LOT
DIVERS LOCAUX
COMMERCIAUX
à LEVALLOIS-PERRET (92)
74, rue Jules Guesde
MISE A PRIX ( ) 600.000 F

à PARIS (17ème)
21, rue des Moines
UNE CHAMBRE
MISE A PRIX : 45.000 F
UN APPARTEMENT

UN S
UNE CAVE et UN EMP
PARIS
8-10-12, p
MISE A PRIX
UN APPA

坚持党的基本路线一百年不动摇
中共深圳市委宣传部
¡Venceremos!

# P

## PÜNKTLICH

## ПУНКТУАЛЬНЫЙ
دقيق
PONTUAL
PUNCTUAL
准时
PONCTUEL
DAKIK
PUNTUAL
几帳面

1509
1510
METERS
OPERATE
EVERY DAY
10 AM TO 8 PM
QUARTERS
ONLY

SIXTY MIN. TIME LIMIT
0 15 30 45 60
QUARTERS ONLY

STAD BRUGGE
PROTON
ELKE DAG / TOUS LES JOURS
JEDEN TAG / EVERY DAY  9.00 - 19.00
TARIEF 1
PARKEERTICKET
MAX = 15 min.
€ 0,05 voor 15 min.
BETALING
MET DE PARKEERAUTOMAAT
(Enkel met munten)
NIET CUMULEERBAAR
TARIEF 2
PARKEERTICKET
MIN = 15 min.
MAX = 2 uur
€ 1,40 per uur
BETALING
MET DE PARKEERAUTOMAAT
(Proton of met munten)
TICKET 15 min.
MAX 2 uur
€ 0,35
GRATIS
TICKET
STOP
TARIEF 3
HALVE DAG TARIE
VAN 9.00 TOT 14.00
VAN 14.00 TOT 19.
€ 12,00
BETALING
BINNEN DE 8 DAGEN VAN
VERZENDINGSDATUM V
BETALINGSUITNODIGING
PER POST WORDT TOEGEST
TICKET
STOP
CALE
KRAUTLI
S.A. KRAUTLI N.V. TEL. 03/481.72.00
KARTE
BARGELD
TARIFFE
CHARGES
TARIFS
TARIF
1/30 min.  Lire 1.000
2/60 min.  Lire 2.500
SELEZIONARE
LA TARIFFA
SELECT CHARGE
SELECTIONNER LE TARIF
TARIF WÄHLEN
INTRODURRE
LA MONETA
O LA TESSERA
INSERT COIN OR CARD
INTRODUCTION MONNAI
OU CARTE
MUNZE ODER
AUSWEISKARTE
EINFUGEN
ESPORRE
IL BIGLIETTO
SUL CRUSCOTTO
SHOW TICKET
ON DASHBOARD
EXPOSER LE BILLET
DANS LA VOITURE
SHEIN AUF
ARMATURENBRETT
AUSTELLEN
ANNULLO CANCELLING
CANCELLATION
HANDLUNG
ALMEX
TESSERE A
SCALARE
"CARTARANCIO"
ATM
TABACCAIO
C.so B. AIRES, 2
30 METRI
LA TESSERA
"CARTARANCIO"
INSERIRE
TESSERE
CARTARANCIO
QUI
SOSTITUISCE
LA MONETA.

# 

# QUIRKY

离奇
**BIZARRE**
**TUHAF**
**EXTRAVAGANTE**
気まぐれ
**SCHRÄG**
**ИЗВОРОТЛИВЫЙ**
مراوغ
**ESQUISITO**

投信口
微讯电话"185"
£15
£33 £16
£32 £16
£8
Litter
AMBULANCIA
SEU
222-3322
dia e noite

PÉRIPHÉRIQUE
SUD
CTIONS
NANCY
METZ

A|C
KENITRA

# R

# RELIGIOUS

宗教
**RELIGIEUX**
**DINDAR**
**RELIGIOSO**
宗教的
**RELIGIÖS**
**РЕЛИГИОЗНЫЙ**
متدين
**RELIGIOSO**

IGREJA
PENTECOSTAL
DEUS É AMOR
769
RIFONDAZIONE
COMUNISTA
SEZ. 7 MARTIRI
SEZ. CASTELLO
7 MARTIRI

JESUS
Medo da morte? JESUS já morreu por você!
Sozinho? JESUS é o melhor am
JT JÓIAS
JT. JÓIAS
295-2986
清真女寺
ان الدين عند الله الاسلام

Durch St. Annas Schutz
und Güte,
uns alle vor Unheil behüte.
1987
1952
BKsM

# R

**RITUALISÉ**

**TÖREN**
**RITUAL**
**儀式**
**RITUELL**
**РИТУАЛЬНЫЙ**
شعائري
**RITUAL**
**RITUALISTIC**
仪式

# R

# ROMÁNTICO

ロマンチック
**ROMANTISCH**
**РОМАНТИЧНЫЙ**
رومانسي
**ROMÂNTICO**
**ROMANTIC**
浪漫
**ROMANTIQUE**
**ROMANTIK**

Bi·Fi
...hat Biß

雲龍 美术装饰部
雲 龍
南七中路
NAN T-ZHONGI U
雲龍美術

空车配货
25931105

# S
# SEGURO

**SAFE**
安全
**SÉCURITAIRE**
**GÜVENLI**
**SEGURO**
安全
**SICHER**
**БЕЗОПАСНЫЙ**
آمن

1639
1640
1641
1642
1643
1644
A
B
C
D
E
F
G
H
I
J
K
L
1639
1640
1641
1642
1643
1644

Das Abstellen
von Fahrrädern
ist untersagt
POLIZEI

Berlin

# S

# SNOBBISH

势利
# SNOB
# ZÜPPE
# ESNOB
俗物
# SNOBISTISCH
# СНОБИСТСКИЙ
مقلد
# SNOBE

VIP
予約車
AIRPORT LIMOUSINE

# S

## SONORO

SONOROUS
洪亮
SONORE
ETKILI
SONORO
格調高く
KLINGEND
ЗВУЧНЫЙ
جهوري

HOTEL
BRIDGE
BRUNA

SSS SIEDLE
GERLING

# S

## SUPER-MEGA

СУПЕР
سوبر
SUPER
SUPER
非常
HYPER
SÜPER
FORMIDABLE
最高

此处禁止停自行车
违者罚款!!!
修车补胎
1.50元
Marlboro

# T

# TEMPORÁRIO

TEMPORARY
临时
TEMPORAIRE
GEÇICI
PROVISIONAL
暂定的
TEMPORÄR
ВРЕМЕННЫЙ
مؤقت

# T

# TRANSFORMED

转变

# TRANSFORMÉ
# BIÇIM DEĞIŞTIRMIŞ
# TRANSFORMADO

変身

# TRANSFORMIERT
# ПРЕВРАЩЕННЫЙ

محول

# TRANSFORMADO

eurosure
INSURANCE COMPANY LTD
Professionally Sure
龍門
LONGMEN
CHINESE
RESTAURANT
andreas shacks constructions ltd

Berliner Kindl
ASIA
ASIA
ASIA-RESTAURANT
LONG
HA LONG
Schülerlotsen
Linien
Köstritzer
PEKING ENTE
CHINA-RESTAURANT
Köstritzer
PEKING ENTE
PEKING ENTE

CHINA RESTAURANT
SIIAN LONG
雙龍酒樓
雙龍酒樓
400
紫禁城大酒樓

RISTORANTE CINESE
SHANGHAI
FAST FOOD
INTERNAZIONALE
LOTUS BLOSSOM
Chinese Restaurant
ALL TAXES INCLUDED

# T

# TRANSPORTABLE

**TAŞINABILIR**
**TRANSPORTABLE**
移動可能
**TRANSPORTABEL**
**ПЕРЕНОСНОЙ**
قابل للنقل
**TRANSPORTÁVEL**
**TRANSPORTABLE**
可运输

回收旧
硒鼓
墨盒
收药
刻字

衣料加工

中国电信 公用电话
CHINA TELECOM
中国电信 公用电话
CHINA TELECOM

CADENA DE TURISMO
ISLAZUL
por toda Cuba
DIVISION VARADERO
ROSSI'S
CREAM
Wall's
Ice Cream
SAARLANDER
"The Real"
SAARLANDER
BEDFORD

HEBREW NATIONAL HOT DOG
HOT DOG
HOT SAUSAGE
HOT PRETZEL
GABILA'S KNISHES
NOVEMBER TRADE-IN SALE
Mit dem Zweiten sieht man besser,
wer bei der WM den Durchblick hat.
Jürgen Klinsmann, ZDF-Experte vor Ort bei der Fußball-WM 2002
ZDF
Cornetto

修
自行车
气管子
拉锁
配钥匙
仿真
富瑶购物店

BALIK EKMEK
750

FUMI
ROYAL

IL WOLF
Relojería
CITIZEN
IL WOLF

Nosso maior
investimento.
BancoRURAL
A evolução do banco.
www.rural.com.br
335-17
www.
DULCERIA
EL
COMANDE
DULCERIA Y LICORES
EN GENERAL

冰爽畅快直透心
冰淇淋
Wall's
知路雪

# T

# TREMBLANT

TITREYEN
TEMBLOROSO
ふるえ
ZITTERND
ДРОЖАЩИЙ
مرتعش
TRÉMULO
TREMBLING
抖动

OTOPARK
PEPSI
ÖZLENEN
BUFE
FLINKOT

**TURISTIK**

**TURÍSTICO**
観光向け
**TOURISTISCH**
**ТУРИСТИЧЕСКИЙ**
سياحي
**TURÍSTICO**
**TOURISTY**
游览
**TOURISTIQUE**

1831
1832
1833
1834
1835
1836
A
B
C
D
E
F
G
H
I
J
K
L
1831
1832
1833
1834
1835
1836

Calvin Klein Jeans
K
CRIB CITY
10 100

# U

**UNIVERSAL**

寰宇
**UNIVERSEL**
**EVRENSEL**
**UNIVERSAL**
ユニバーサル
**UNIVERSAL**
**УНИВЕРСАЛЬНЫЙ**
عالمي
**UNIVERSAL**

1849
1850
1851
1852
1853
1854
A
B
C
D
E
F 
G
H
I
J
K
L 
1849
1850
1851
1852
1853
1854

# U

## UNSICHTBAR

НЕВИДИМЫЙ
غير مرئي
INVISÍVEL
UNSEEN
无形
INVISIBLE
GÖRÜLMEMIŞ
INVISIBLE
見えざる

1867
1868
1869
1870
1871
1872
A
B
C
D
E
F
G
H
I
J
K
L
1867
1868
1869
1870
1871
1872

DEFENSE D'AFFICHER
DEFENSE D'AFFICHER

1879
1880
1881
1882
1883
1884
A
B
C
D
E
F
G
H
I
J
K
L

送 水 口
（消防隊専用）
非 常 電 話

1903
1904
1905
1906
1907
1908
A
B
C
D
E
F
G
H
I
J
K
L
1903
1904
1905
1906
1907
1908

# U

## URGENT

**ACIL**
**URGENTE**
緊急
**DRINGEND**
**СРОЧНЫЙ**
عاجل
**URGENTE**
**URGENT**
紧急

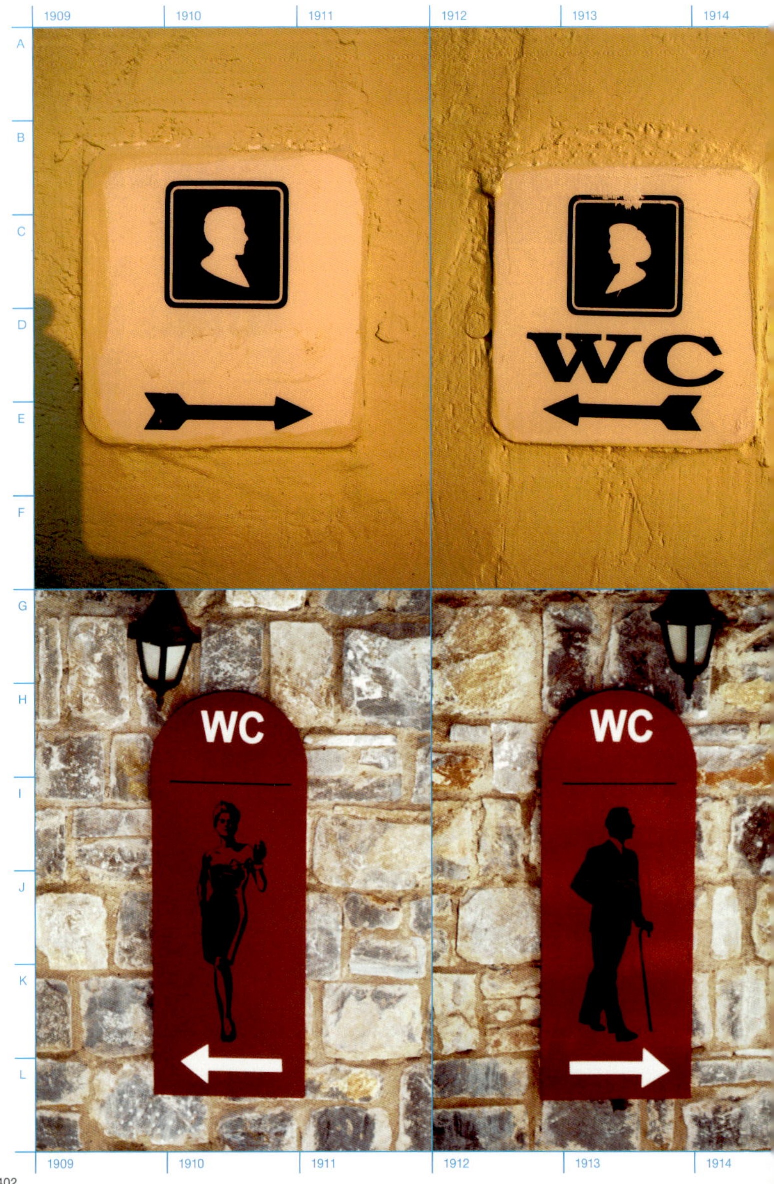

WC
WC
WC

سيدات
LADIES
رجال
MEN

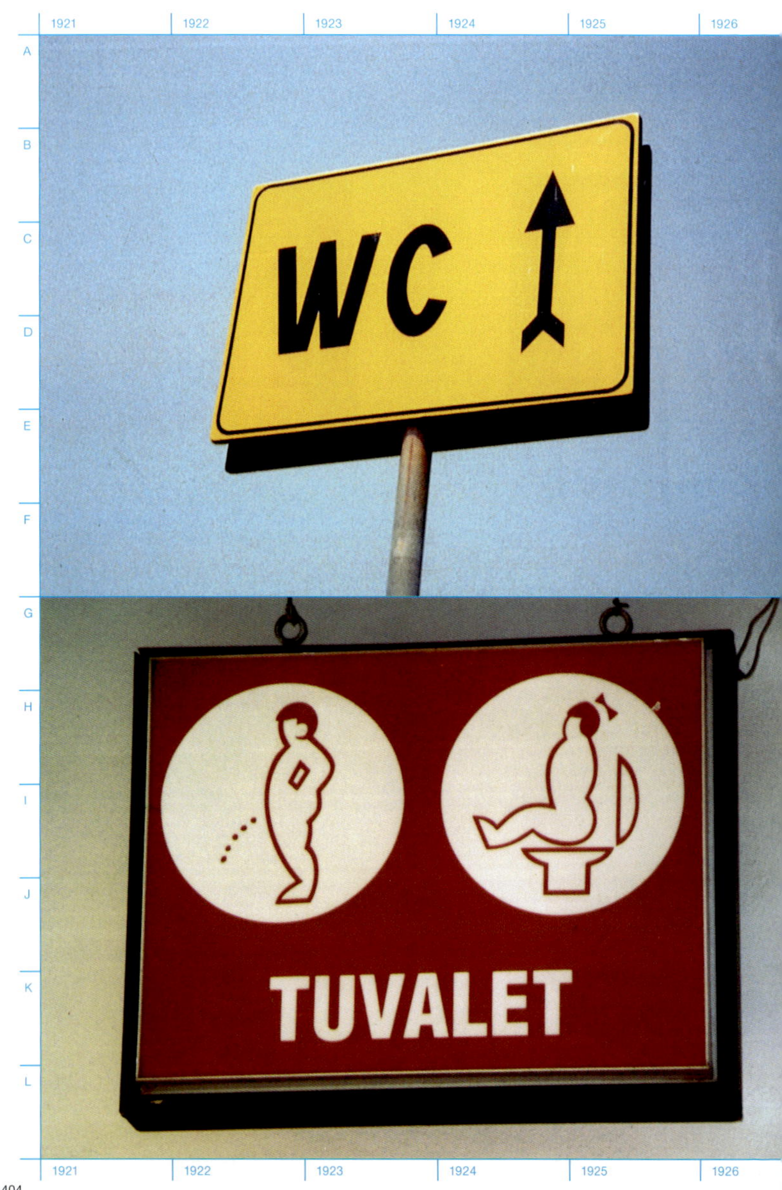

WC
TUVALET

WC
MODERN
WC
TATSAN

WC 公共厕所

WC
ÇARŞI
İÇİNDE

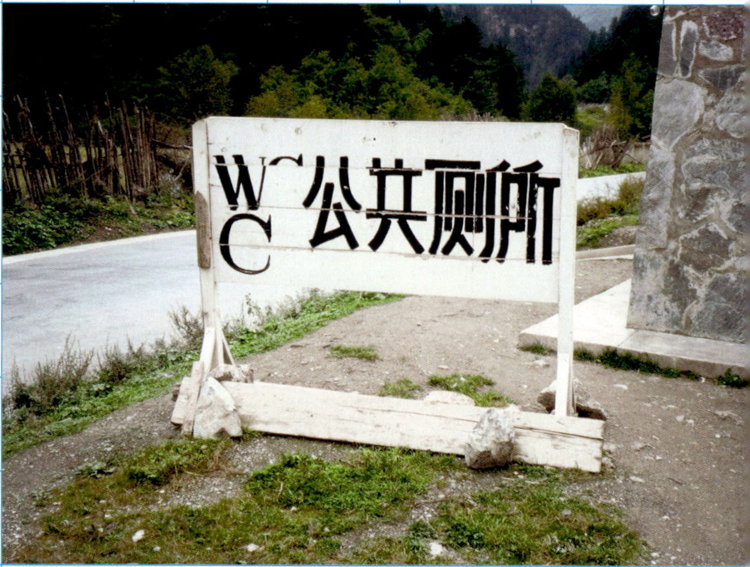

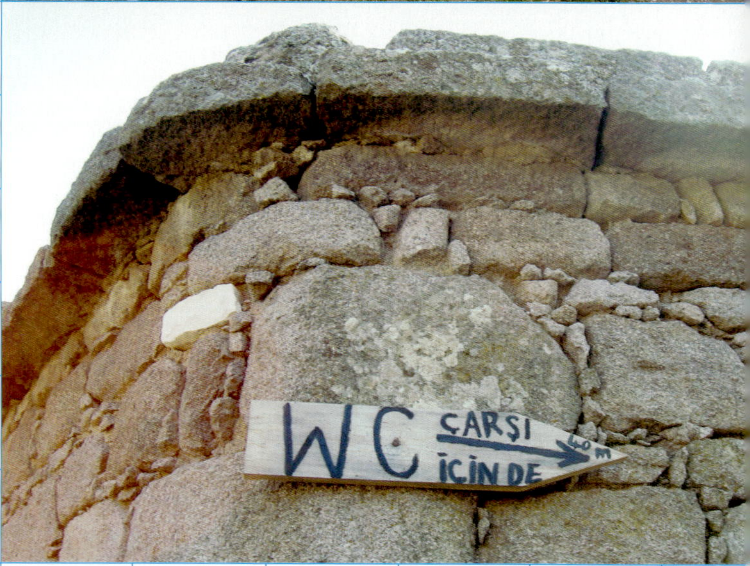

WC
an der
Thomas-
kirche
Öffentliche Toilettenanlage
Geöffnet 10.00 bis 18.00 Uhr

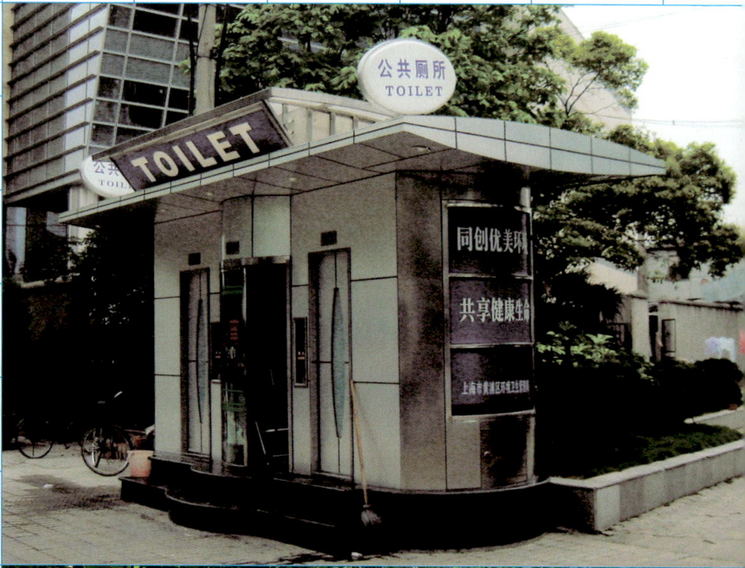

公共厕所
TOILET
TOILET
公共
TOI
同创优美环境
共享健康生命
上海市黄浦区环卫电卫生管理所

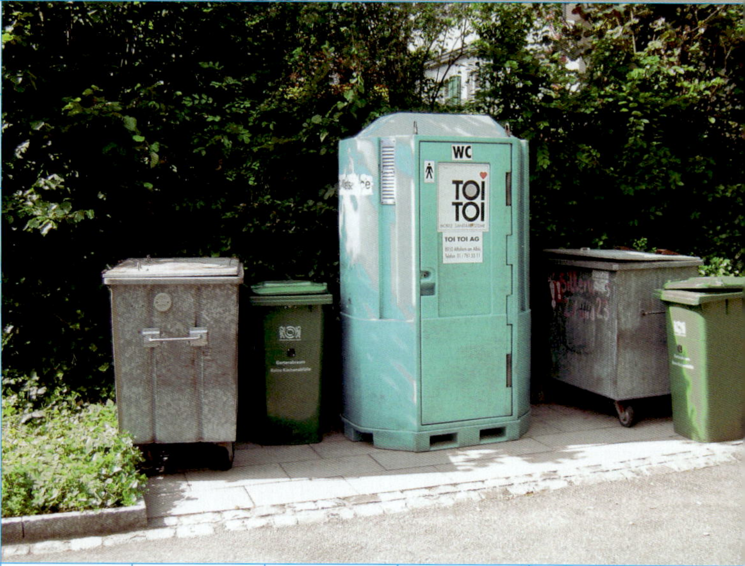

WC
TOI
TOI
TOI TOI AG

Toilette
CITY TOILETTE

WC

# V

# VERBORGEN

СПРЯТАННЫЙ
مخفي
OCULTO
HIDDEN
隐藏
SECRET
GIZLI
OCULTO
秘匿

1975
1976
1977
1978
1979
1980
A
B
C
D
E
F
G
H
I
J
K
L
71
73
77
79
1975
1976
1977
1978
1979
1980

134

BIBLIOTECA CIVICA
"ARCARI"

# V

# VERBOTEN

ЗАПРЕЩЕННЫЙ
ممنوع
PROIBIDO
FORBIDDEN
禁止
INTERDIT
YASAK
PROHIBIDO
禁じ手

GIRILMEZ
NO ENTRY
请勿入内
请勿停车
IMPASSE PRIVEE
STATIONNEMENT
INTERDIT

S.E.C.A.R.A.C.
1 2
RESERVE
Street Drinking
Prohibited
Drinking alcohol or
carrying it in an
open container could
result in confiscation
and/or a fine
Brighton & Hove
saferstreets
GÜVENLİK
KEMERİNİ TAK
NO
PARKING
Plätze gesperrt
Campi chiusi
Canchas cerradas
Terrains fermés

NO PARKING TUESDAY
5pm – 12m
POLICE DEPARTMENT
NO PARKIN
AT ANYTIM
Verbot!
Das Ablagern von Material aller Art ist für jedermann untersagt.
Liegenschaftenverwaltung der Stadt Zürich
GASFLASCHENLAGER RAUCHEN VERBOTEN
NO
ALCOHOL
BEYOND
THIS POINT
BRIGHTON PIER
It is dangerous & forbidden to jump, dive or swim from the pier.
Rauchen
und Umgang mit Feuer im Umkreis von 5 m polizeilich verboten!
ZONA MILITARE
LIMITE INVALICABILE
MILITÄRZONE
UNPASSIERBARE GRENZE

Verlassen des
Weges ist verboten.
Id es scumandà da
bandunar la senda
为保庙内安全清洁
请敬烧三支香
禁止烧成把香
Baden
verboten
IL EST DEFENDU
D'ENTRER DANS LE JARDIN
AVEC DES FLEURS
A LA MAIN

JEAN PAULHAN

BEACH INSTRUCTION
تعليمـــات الـشـــاطئ

Please Do Not Swim After Sunset.
لسلامتكم يرجى عدم السباحة بعد غروب الشمس.

Please Do Not Swim If Red Flag Is Raised.
يرجى عدم السباحة في حالة رفع العلم الأحمر.

Please Do Not Swim At Current Areas Or Close To The Rocks.
يرجى عدم السباحة عند الصخور وفي مناطق التيارات البحرية.

Children Are The Responsibility Of Their Accompanying Adult.
مسؤولية الأطفال تقع على المرافقين الكبار.

Please Conserve Marine & Terrestrial Environment & Do Not Damage It.
يرجى المحافظة على البيئة البحرية والبرية وعدم المساس بها أو إتلافها.

Please Keep The Beach Clean & Do Not Leave Garbage.
يرجى المحافظة على النظافة وعدم ترك المخلفات على الـشـاطئ.

No Pets Allowed On The Beach.
لا يسمح باصطحاب الحيوانات إلى الـشـاطئ.

No Barbecue Or Using Fire Or Camping On The Beach.
لا يسمح بالشواء أو إشعال النار على الـشـاطئ.

The Administration Will Not Be Responsible For Any Personal Accident Or Theft Negligence.
الإدارة غير مسؤولة عن أية حوادث شخصية أو سرقات أو إهـمـال.

Legal Action Will Be Taken For Not Complying With The Above Instruction.
مخالفة التعليمات أعلاه تعرضكم للمسائلة والإجراءات القانونية.

THANK YOU
شــكـــراً لكـــم

www.publicparks@dm.gov.ae

Urinieren verboten

Videoüberwachter Bereich
Es wird gebeten
vor der
Kirchenfassade
nicht zu
musizieren.

# V

# VICE VERSA

**VICE VERSA**
反之亦然
**VICE VERSA**
**TAM TERSI**
**VICEVERSA**
逆もあり
**VICE VERSA**
**НАОБОРОТ**
والعكس

VIPROSERSA
5780
CAFE BA

KEBAB

2047
2048
2049
2050
2051
2052
A
B
C
D
E
F
G
H
I
J
K
L
2047
2048
2049
2050
2051
2052

# V

# VOILÉ

**ÖRTÜLÜ**
**VELADO**
秘密のベール
**VERHÜLLT**
**ЗАВУАЛИРОВАННЫЙ**
محجوب
**VELADO**
**VEILED**
遮掩

2060
2061
2062
2063
2064
A
B
C
D
E
F
G
H
I
J
K
L
2060
2061
2062
2063
2064

# V

# VULNÉRABLE

**SAVUNMASIZ**
**VULNERABLE**
脆弱
**VERLETZLICH**
**УЯЗВИМЫЙ**
عرضة للانتقاد
**VULNERÁVEL**
**VULNERABLE**
脆弱

FRONTIÈRES
REV'ETHNIC

ΚΙΝΔΥΝΟΣ
ΑΝ
ΑΤΟ

自転車を除く
BOUCHERIE COMESTIBLES

ΑΝΘΟΠΩΛΕΙΟ
FLOWER SHOP
Elysée
ΑΝΘΟΠΩΛΕΙΟ
FLOWER SHOP

# W

**WARTEND**

**ОЖИДАЮЩИЙ**

منتظر

**À ESPERA**

**WAITING**

等待

**EN ATTENTE**

**BEKLEYEN**

**ESPERANDO**

待機

2108 2109 2110 2111 2112

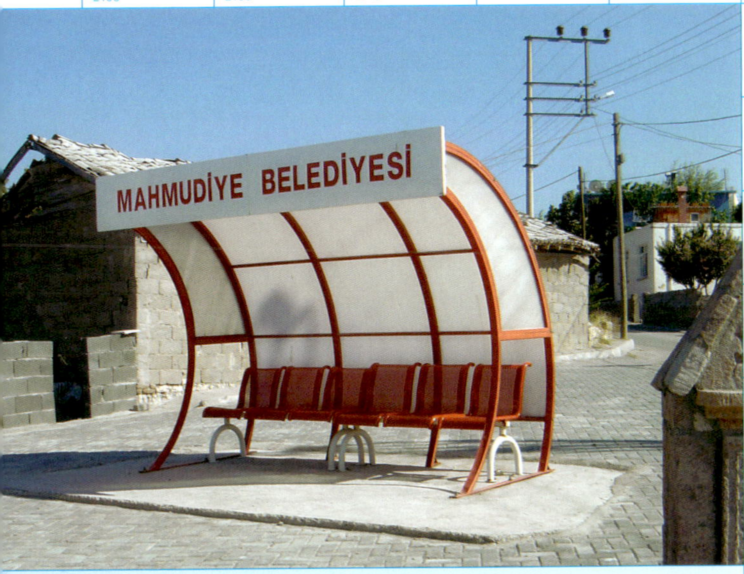
MAHMUDİYE BELEDİYESİ

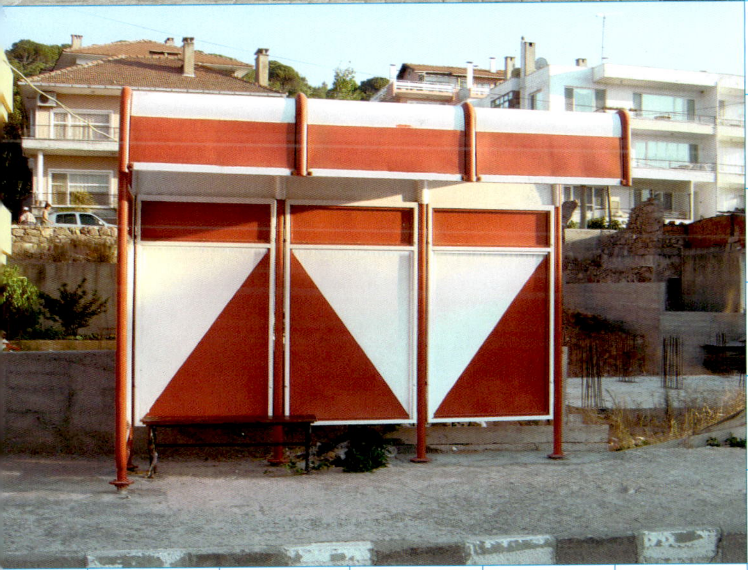

A B C D E F G H I J K L

2108 2109 2110 2111 2112

# W

## WAS IST DAS?

ЧТО ЭТО?

ما هذا؟

O QUE É?

WHAT IS IT?

这是什么？

QU'EST-CE?

BU NEDIR?

¿QUÉ ES?

これは何？

# X-MAL

**X PA3**
× مرات
**N VEZES**
**X-TIMES**
多次
**FRÉQUENT**
**BILINMEYEN ZAMANLAR**
**X VECES**
幾度となく

REGGAE
DA BASE AT SCARLETT NIGHLIFE CENTER, ARCHSTRASSE 8, WINTERTHUR
kakan
Salonu
ipekçi
Gü
Spor
istanb

DEFENSE D'AFFICHER          LOI DU 29 JUILLET 188
PULSIONS     billboard
La liberté d'expression est née sur les murs.
Les afficheurs.
EFENSE D'AFFICHER          LOI DU 2

# Y

## YELLOW

黄色
JAUNE
SARI
AMARILLO
黄色
GELB
ЖЕЛТЫЙ
أصفر
AMARELO

SOKKEN
PER PA
B.I.
Warnung Diebe !
Beware Of Thieves !
Attention aux voleurs !
Police Information
VORSICHT !

TAXI TAXI
PAPERS
2
5
0
0
0
1
2
3
0
0
0
1
1
NEXT
3 km
Wege und Treppen
verden bei Eisglätt
oder
nach Schneefall
nicht abgestreut
Betreten erfolgt
auf eigene Gefahr.
Magistrat
der Stadt Darmstadt
PIETONS
DIEBE

2155
2156
2157
2158
2159
2160
A
B
C
D
E
F
G
H
I
J
K
L
2155
2156
2157
2158
2159
2160

# Z

# ZEBRA-STRIPED

斑马纹
**ZÉBRÉ**
**ZEBRA-DESENLI**
**RAYADO**
縞模様
**GESTREIFT**
**ПОЛОСАТЫЙ**
مخطط كالحمار الوحشي
**LISTRADO**

HOCHTIEF

即
停
即
落
即
走
→
滿

BAR PURO

# Z

## ZEITGENÖSSISCH

СОВРЕМЕННЫЙ

معاصر

CONTEMPORÂNEO

CONTEMPORARY

当代

CONTEMPORAIN

ÇAĞDAŞ

CONTEMPORÁNEO

現代風

ANZEIG
M. Pech
Sanitätsfachhandel
Orthopädie-Technik
Medizintechnik
Ihr Partner
in allen Stadtteilen
DE FRANCE

Schweppes
Sonnenhaus
Rudolf Ziegler
Buchhandlung
Kunsthandwerk
Heidrun Klinkmann
Oranienburger Str. 1
O-Berlin 1020
☎ 2 82 31 89
150 Meter von hier
HOTEL
KASTANIENHOF

CASINO INTERLAKEN
SUNRISE
SUNSET

# Z

## ZWECKLOS

БЕСПОЛЕЗНЫЙ
بلا فائدة
INÚTIL
USELESS
无用
INUTILE
YARARSIZ
INÚTIL
役立たず

# A



# F



# K



# B



# G



# L



# C



# H



# M



# D



# I



# N



# E



# J



# O

# P



# Q



# R



# S



# T



# U



# V



# W



# X



# Y



# Z

# A

**ACHTUNG**
**ВНИМАНИЕ**
**ATENÇÃO**
**ATTENTION**
注意
**ATTENTION**
انتبه
**DIKKAT**
**ATENCIÓN**
注意



# A

**AUTOMÁTICO**
**AUTOMATIC**
自动
**AUTOMATIQUE**
**OTOMATIK**
**AUTOMÁTICO**
オートマチック
**AUTOMATISCH**
**АВТОМАТИЧЕСКИЙ**
آلي



# A

**AUTORITAIRE**
**OTORITER**
**AUTORITARIO**
権威主義
**AUTORITÄR**
**АВТОРИТАРНЫЙ**
ديكتاتوري
**AUTORITÁRIO**
**AUTHORITARIAN**
独裁



# B

**BEZAUBERND**
**ПЛЕНИТЕЛЬНЫЙ**
بي وتشنج
**FASCINANTE**
**BEWITCHING**
迷人
**CHARMANT**
**BÜYÜLEYICI**
**PRECIOSO**
魅惑



# B

**BRANCHÉ**
**DEMET**
**CONECTADO**
束
**VERKABELT**
**ВКЛЮЧЕННЫЙ В ЦЕПЬ**
في حزمة
**LIGADO**
**WIRED**
成捆



# C

**CALIENTE**
灼熱
**BRANDHEISS**
**ЖГУЧИЙ**
ساخن كالفحم
**EM BRASA**
**COAL-HOT**
炽热
**BRÛLANT**
**KOR ATEŞI**



# C

**COMPLEX**
复杂
**COMPLEXE**
**KOMPLEKS**
**COMPLEJO**
複雑
**KOMPLEX**
**СЛОЖНЫЙ**
مركب
**COMPLEXO**



# C

**CONCENTRADO**
**CONCENTRATED**
集中
**CONCENTRÉ**
**KONSANTRE**
**CONCENTRADO**
集中
**KONZENTRIERT**
**КОНЦЕНТРИРОВАННЫЙ**
مركز

# C

**CONTRADICTORY**
矛盾
**CONTRADICTOIRE**
**ZIT**
**CONTRADICTORIO**
矛盾
**WIDERSPRÜCHLICH**
**ПРОТИВОРЕЧИВЫЙ**
متناقض
**CONTRADITÓRIO**



# C

**CONTRÔLÉ**
**KONTROLLU**
**CONTROLADO**
コントロール
**KONTROLLIERT**
**КОНТРОЛИРУЕМЫЙ**
مراقب
**CONTROLADO**
**CONTROLLED**
控制



# D

**DECORATIVO**
あでやか
**DEKORATIV**
**ДЕКОРАТИВНЫЙ**
مزين
**DECORATIVO**
**DECORATIVE**
装饰
**DÉCORATIF**
**DEKORATIF**





# D

**DESIGNED**
**СПРОЕКТИРОВАННЫЙ**
مصمم
**DESENHADO**
**DESIGNED**
设计
**CONÇU**
**TASARLANMIŞ**
**DISEÑADO**
デザイン



# D

**DIRECTIF**
**YÖNLENDIREN**
**DIRIGIENDO**
方向づけ
**DIREKTIV**
**НАПРАВЛЯЮЩИЙ**
توجيه
**DIRECTIVO**
**DIRECTING**
指导



# D

**DISCRETO**
**DISCREET**
道慎
**DISCRET**

**SAĞDUYULU**
**DISCRETO**
控えめ
**DISKRET**
**СДЕРЖАННЫЙ**
حكيم



# E

**ELECTED**
选举
**ÉLECTORAL**
**SEÇILMIŞ**
**ELEGIDO**
選出
**ERWÄHLT**
**ИЗБРАННЫЙ**
منتخب
**ELEITO**



# E

**ÉLECTRIFIÉ**
**ELEKTRIKLENMIŞ**
**ELECTRIFICADO**
感電
**ELEKTRIFIZIERT**
**ЭЛЕКТРИФИЦИРОВАННЫЙ**
مكهرب
**ELECTRIFICADO**
**ELECTRIFIED**
带电



# E

**ENCODED**
编码
**CODIFIÉ**
**ŞIFRELI**
**CODIFICADO**
暗号
**VERSCHLÜSSELT**
**ЗАШИФРОВАННЫЙ**
مشفر
**CODIFICADO**

# E

**ENVAHISSANT**
**DAVETSIZ**
**INVASOR**
でしゃばり
**VERDRÄNGEND**
**ВТОРГАЮЩИЙСЯ**
متطفل
**INVASIVO**
**INTRUSIVE**
侵入

511 A Dailing
517 A Frankfurt
517G New York
523 A London*
523 E s'Gravenhage
523 I London*
525 E London
525 I Nicosia
527 A Frankfurt
527 E Barcelone
527 I Copenhagen
529 A London*
529 E Figline
529 I Casablanca
531 A London*
531 E London*
533 A London*
533 E London*
533 I Palma de Mallorca
535 A Siena
535 E London
535 I Lyon
537 A London*
537 E London*
539 A Interlaken
539 E Zurich
539 I Zurich
541 A London*
541 E Darmstadt
541 I Zurich
543 A Leipzig
543 I Montreuil
545 I Marseille
547 A London*

# E

**EXTROVERTIDO**
外交的
**EXTROVERTIERT**
**ЭКСТРАВЕРТНЫЙ**
منبسط
**EXTROVERTIDO**
**EXTROVERTED**
外向
**EXTRAVERTI**
**DIŞA DÖNÜK**

553 A Shanghai
565 A Istanbul

# F

**FEUCHT**
**ВЛАЖНЫЙ**
رطب
**HÚMIDO**
**DAMP**
潮湿
**HUMIDE**
**NEMLI**
**HÚMEDO**
湿气

583 A Paris
589 A Paris
595 A Izmir
595 G Platres
601 A Beijing
607 A Zuoz

# G

**GEDULDIG**
**ТЕРПЕЛИВЫЙ**
صبور
**PACIENTE**
**PATIENT**
耐心
**PATIENT**
**HASTA**
**PACIENTE**
忍耐

613 A Paris
625 A Montreuil
625 E Müllheim
625 I Maastricht
627 A Cadaques
627 E Iràklion
629 A Bregenz
629 E Stockholm
629 I Townsville*
631 A Istanbul
631 E Venice
631 I Monaco
633 A Palma de Mallorca
633 E Copenhagen
633 I Lisbon*
635 A Casablanca
635 E London
635 I Budapest
637 A Offenbach
637 G Paris

# G

**GESCHWÄTZIG**
**БОЛТЛИВЫЙ**
ثرثار
**FALADOR**
**GARRULOUS**
喋喋不休
**BAVARD**

**BOŞBOĞAZ**
**HABLADOR**
多井

643 A Basel
649 A Suzhun
649 G Shanghai
652 A Shenyang
652 G Shanghai
655 A Beijing
655 G Ayvalik
658 A Denpassar
658 G Osaka
661 A Shenzhen
661 G London*
664 G Prague
667 A New York
673 A Chengdu
679 A Stockholm

# G

**GIGANTESCO**
**GIGANTIC**
巨大
**GIGANTESQUE**
**DEVASA**
**GIGANTESCO**
巨大
**GIGANTISCH**
**ГИГАНТСКИЙ**
ضخم

685 A Las Vegas
691 A Leipzig
697 A São Paulo
697 G Berlin
703 A Brazil
703 G Shanghai
709 A Offenbach

# G

**GLOBAL**
全球
**GLOBAL**
**GLOBAL**
**GLOBAL**
グローバル
**GLOBAL**
**ГЛОБАЛЬНЫЙ**
عالمي
**GLOBAL**

715 A La Alcadia
715 G Kobe
721 G Prague
727 G Osaka
733 A Kyoto
733 G Fez
739 A Bel Horizonte
745 A Montreal
745 G Nicosia
748 A Nicosia

748 G Bergama
751 A Nicosia
751 G Shanghai

# G

**GRÜN**
**ЗЕЛЕНЫЙ**
أخضر
**VERDE**
**GREEN**
绿色
**VERT**
**YEŞIL**
**VERDE**
绿

757 A Darmstadt
757 G Stuttgart
760 A Chengdu
760 G Casablanca
763 A Techirdag
763 G Shanghai
766 A Meknes
766 G Beijing
769 A Natal

# H

**HARMONIOSO**
調和
**HARMONISCH**
**ГАРМОНИЧНЫЙ**
ملاءمة
**HARMÓNICO**
**HARMONIZING**
和谐
**HARMONIEUX**
**UYUMLU**

775 A Xuanhua
781 A Istanbul
787 A Paris

# H

**HERMÉTIQUE**
**BÜYÜSEL**
**HERMÉTICO**
密封
**HERMETISCH**
**ГЕРМЕТИЧЕСКИЙ**
سحري
**HERMÉTICO**
**HERMETIC**
封闭

793 A Frankfurt
793 G Frankfurt
799 A Frankfurt
799 G Frankfurt
808 A Frankfurt
811 A Lisbon
817 A Bern

# H

**HIMMLISCH**
**АНГЕЛЬСКИЙ**
سماوي
**ANGÉLICO**
**HEAVENLY**
天堂
**DIVIN**
**HARIKA**
**ANGELICAL**
至福

823 A Berlin
835 A Venice

# H

**HUMANO**
人
**MENSCHLICH**
**ЧЕЛОВЕЧНЫЙ**
إنساني
**HUMANO**
**HUMAN**
人类
**HUMAIN**
**İNSAN**

841 A Dresden
841 G Shanghai
847 A Bel Horizonte
847 D Beijing
847 G Baden
847 J Cartageno
850 A Amsterdam
850 D Müllheim
850 G Recife
850 J Darmstadt
853 A Weimar
859 A Paris
859 D Paris
859 G Paris
862 A Paris
862 D Nice
862 G Padua
862 J Leipzig
865 A Nicosia
865 G Kassel
871 G Milan
874 A Nicosia
874 D Palma de Mallorca
874 G Bel Horizonte
877 A Shanghai

# I

**INSEPARABLE**
不可分离
**INSÉPARABLE**
**AYRILMAZ**
**INSEPARABLE**
分離不可

**UNZERTRENNLICH**
**НЕОТДЕЛИМЫЙ**
لا يمكن فصله
**INSEPARÁVEL**

883 A Essen
889 A Zurich
895 A Shanghai

# J

**JEUNE ET JOLIE**
**GENÇ VE GÜZEL**
**JÓVENES Y GUAPAS**
若く美しく
**JUNG UND SCHÖN**
**МОЛОДЫЕ И КРАСИВЫЕ**
شاب وجميل
**JOVENS E BONITAS**
**YOUNG AND PRETTY**
年轻貌美

901 A Myra*
901 D Bel Horizonte
901 G Lugano
901 J Hamburg
902 D Shenzhen
902 G Bern
902 J Hamburg
904 A Fez
904 G Beijing
905 A Dubai*
905 D Osaka
905 G Beijing
905 J Oostende*
907 A Cologne
907 D Suzhou
907 J Beijing
908 A Tourcoing
908 G New York
908 J Hamburg
910 A Basel
910 D Leipzig
910 G Shanghai
910 J Frankfurt
911 A Valencia*
911 G Zurich
911 J Frankfurt
913 A Prague
913 G Sankt Gallen
919 A Dessau
919 G Shenyang
925 A Leipzig
931 A Lisbon
931 G Fez
937 A Bel Horizonte
937 G Bel Horizonte
940 A Bel Horizonte
940 G Bel Horizonte
943 A Bel Horizonte
943 G Bel Horizonte
949 A Paris
949 G Paris

**MOBILE**
**MOBIL**
**MÓVIL**
移動式
**MOBIL**
**МОБИЛЬНЫЙ**
متنقّل



# N

**NOMMÉ**
**ADI GEÇEN**
**NOMINADO**
指名
**NÄMLICH**
**НАЗВАННЫЙ**
محدد
**NOMEADO**
**NAMED**
命名



# N

**NUMEROUS**
众多
**NOMBREUX**
**ÇOK**
**NUMEROSO**
大群
**ZAHLREICH**
**МНОГОЧИСЛЕННЫЙ**
عديد
**NUMEROSO**



# N

**NUTRITIOUS**
营养
**NOURRISSANT**
**BESLEYICI**
**NUTRITIVO**
栄養豊富
**NAHRHAFT**
**ПИТАТЕЛЬНЫЙ**
مغذي
**NUTRITIVO**



# O

**OMNIPRÉSENT**
**HAZIR VE NAZIR**
**OMNIPRESENTE**
偏在
**ALLGEGENWÄRTIG**
**ВЕЗДЕСУЩИЙ**
كلي الوجود
**OMNIPRESENTE**
**OMNIPRESENT**
无处不在





# O

**ORNAMENTAL**
**ORNAMENTAL**
装潢
**ORNEMENTAL**
**SÜSLEYICI**
**ORNAMENTAL**
飾りもの
**ORNAMENTAL**
**ДЕКОРАТИВНЫЙ**
زخرفي



# P

**PLANO**
自然回帰
**BODENSTÄNDIG**
**ПРОСТОЙ**
واقعي
**COMESINHO**
**DOWN-TO-EARTH**
朴实

**TERRE À TERRE**
**AYAĞI YERE BASAN**
1369 A Palma de Mallorca
1375 A New York
1381 A Berlin
1381 G Hamburg
1387 A Amsterdam
1387 G Prague
1393 A San Francisco
1399 A Bern
1405 A Leipzig
1405 D Frankfurt
1405 G Rome
1405 J Lisbon
1408 A Rabat
1408 D Paris
1408 G Paris
1408 J Padova
1417 A London
1417 D London
1417 G London
1417 J London
1420 A London
1420 D London
1420 G London
1420 J London

# P

**PRIVAT**
**ЧАСТНЫЙ**
خاص
**PRIVADO**
**PRIVATE**
隱私
**PRIVÉ**
**ÖZEL**
**PRIVADO**
私的
1423 A Zurich
1423 G Baden-Baden

# P

**PROTECTED**
保护
**PROTÉGÉ**
**KORUMALI**
**PROTEGIDO**
保護
**BESCHÜTZT**
**ЗАЩИЩЕННЫЙ**
محمي
**PROTEGIDO**
1429 A Cologne
1429 G Milan
1435 A Prague
1435 G Prague
1441 A Bel Horizonte
1441 G Bel Horizonte
1444 A Bel Horizonte

1444 G Bel Horizonte
1447 A Basel
1453 A Montreuil
1453 G New York
1456 A New York
1456 G Zurich
1459 A Paris
1465 A Rotterdam

# P

**PROTESTATAIRE**
**PROTESTO**
**PROTESTANDO**
抗議
**PROTESTIEREND**
**ПРОТЕСТУЮЩИЙ**

**CONTESTATÁRIO**
**PROTESTING**
抗议
1471 A Berlin
1471 G Berlin
1477 A Berlin
1477 G Berlin
1483 A Cadaques
1483 G Paris
1489 A Bern
1489 G Istanbul
1495 A Paris

# P

**PROVISIONAL**
即興
**PROVISORISCH**
**ВРЕМЕННЫЙ**
ارتجالي
**IMPROVISADO**
**IMPROVISED**
即兴
**PROVISOIRE**
**DOĞAÇLAMA**
1501 A Istanbul

# P

**PUBLIC**
**HALK**
**PÚBLICO**
公的
**ÖFFENTLICH**
**ПУБЛИЧНЫЙ**
عام
**PÚBLICO**
**PUBLIC**
公共
1507 A Paris
1513 G Paris
1519 A Shenzen
1519 G La Habana

# P

**PÜNKTLICH**
**ПУНКТУАЛЬНЫЙ**
دقيق
**PONTUAL**
**PUNCTUAL**
准时
**PONCTUEL**
**DAKIK**
**PUNTUAL**
几帳面
1525 A Zurich
1525 G Zurich
1528 A Frankfurt
1528 G San Francisco
1537 A Neuland
1540 A Brugge*
1540 G Dubai*

# Q

**QUIRKY**
离奇
**BIZARRE**
**TUHAF**
**EXTRAVAGANTE**
気まぐれ
**SCHRÄG**
**ИЗВОРОТЛИВЫЙ**
مراوغ
**ESQUISITO**
1543 A Chengdu
1543 G Iràklion
1546 A London*
1546 G Bel Horizonte
1549 A Lisbon
1549 G Lyon
1552 A New York
1552 G Leipzig
1555 A Tourcoing
1555 G Casablanca

# R

**RELIGIOUS**
宗教
**RELIGIEUX**
**DINDAR**
**RELIGIOSO**
宗教的
**RELIGIÖS**
**РЕЛИГИОЗНЫЙ**
متدين
**RELIGIOSO**
1561 A Bel Horizonte
1561 G Venice
1567 A Bel Horizonte
1567 G Shanghai

# R

**RITUALISÉ**
**TÖREN**
**RITUAL**
儀式
**RITUELL**
**РИТУАЛЬНЫЙ**
شعائري
**RITUAL**
**RITUALISTIC**
仪式
1579 A Paris

# R

**ROMÁNTICO**
ロマンチック
**ROMANTISCH**
**РОМАНТИЧНЫЙ**
رومانسي
**ROMÂNTICO**
**ROMANTIC**
浪漫
**ROMANTIQUE**
**ROMANTIK**
1585 A Rabat
1585 G Barcelone
1591 A Cienfuegos
1591 G s'Gravenhage
1597 A Nicosia
1597 G Monaco
1597 J Barcelone
1600 A Venice
1600 D Mannheim
1600 G Bern
1600 J Paris
1603 D London
1603 G Bel Horizonte
1603 J Tourcoing
1606 A Leipzig
1606 G Venice
1606 J Bremen
1609 A Istanbul
1615 A Trinidad
1621 A Reschen/Resia
1621 G Prague
1624 A Bel Horizonte
1624 G Bern
1627 A Ticino
1627 G Shenyang
1630 A Fez
1630 G Zuoz
1633 A Shenyang

# S

**SEGURO**
**SAFE**
安全
**SÉCURITAIRE**

**GÜVENLI**
**SEGURO**
安全
**SICHER**
**БЕЗОПАСНЫЙ**
آمن
1639 A Bern
1639 D Paris
1639 G Venice
1639 J Paris
1642 D Paris
1642 G Paris
1642 J Berlin
1645 A Paris
1642 G Paris
1648 A Paris
1648 G Paris
1651 A Leipzig
1651 G Leipzig
1657 A Leipzig
1663 A Leipzig

# S

**SNOBBISH**
势利
**SNOB**
**ZÜPPE**
**ESNOB**
俗物
**SNOBISTISCH**
**СНОБИСТСКИЙ**
مقلّد
**SNOBE**
1669 A Osaka

# S

**SONORO**
**SONOROUS**
洪亮
**SONORE**
**ETKILI**
**SONORO**
格調高く
**KLINGEND**
**ЗВУЧНЫЙ**
جهوري
1675 A Venice
1675 G Venice
1678 A Venice
1678 G Venice
1681 A Venice
1681 G Venice
1684 A Venice
1684 G Venice
1687 A Paris

# S

**SUPER-MEGA**
**СУПЕР**
سوبر
**SUPER**
**SUPER**
非常
**HYPER**
**SÜPER**
**FORMIDABLE**
最高
1693 A Shenyang
1693 G Shenyabg
1696 A Shenyang
1696 G Rabat

# T

**TEMPORÁRIO**
**TEMPORARY**
临时
**TEMPORAIRE**
**GEÇICI**
**PROVISIONAL**
暂定的
**TEMPORÄR**
**ВРЕМЕННЫЙ**
مؤقت
1699 A Zurich
1705 A Zurich
1705 D Zurich
1705 G Zurich
1705 J Zurich
1706 A Zurich
1706 D Zurich
1706 G Zurich
1706 J Zurich
1708 A Zurich
1708 D Zurich
1708 G Zurich
1708 J Zurich
1709 A Zurich
1709 D Zurich
1709 G Zurich
1709 J Zurich
1711 A Zurich

# T

**TRANSFORMED**
转变
**TRANSFORMÉ**
**BIÇIM DEĞIŞTIRMIŞ**
**TRANSFORMADO**
变身
**TRANSFORMIERT**
**ПРЕВРАЩЕННЫЙ**
محول
**TRANSFORMADO**
1717 A Nicosia

1729 A Berlin
1729 G Leipzig
1735 A Zurich
1735 G Lille
1741 A Ticino
1741 G San Francisco
1744 A Perugia
1744 G San Francisco

# T

**TRANSPORTABLE**
**TAŞINABILIR**
**TRANSPORTABLE**
移動可能
**TRANSPORTABEL**
**ПЕРЕНОСНОЙ**
قابل للنقل
**TRANSPORTÁVEL**
**TRANSPORTABLE**
可运输
1747 A Shenyang
1747 G Phocaea
1753 A Wuxi
1753 G Fez
1759 A Shenyang
1759 G Shanghai
1765 A Shanghai
1765 G Shanghai
1771 A Varadero
1771 G London
1777 A New York
1777 G Berlin
1783 A Shenyang
1783 G Shenyang
1789 A Assos
1795 A Bogotà
1807 A Bel Horizonte
1807 G Bogotà
1813 A Zhangzhou
1813 G Chengdu

# T

**TREMBLANT**
**TITREYEN**
**TEMBLOROSO**
ふるえ
**ZITTERND**
**ДРОЖАЩИЙ**
مرتعش
**TRÉMULO**
**TREMBLING**
抖动
1825 A Ayvalik

# T

**TURISTIK**
**TURÍSTICO**
観光向け

**TOURISTISCH**
**ТУРИСТИЧЕСКИЙ**
سياحي
**TURÍSTICO**
**TOURISTY**
游览
**TOURISTIQUE**
1831 A Venice
1831 E Venice
1831 I Venice
1833 A Venice
1833 E Venice
1833 I Venice
1835 A Venice
1835 E Venice
1835 I Venice
1837 A Darmstadt
1837 E Cologne
1837 I s'Gravenhage
1839 A Istanbul*
1839 E New York
1839 I Rom
1841 A Frankfurt
1841 E Oostende*
1841 I Nice
1843 A Paris

# U

**UNIVERSAL**
寰宇
**UNIVERSEL**
**EVRENSEL**
**UNIVERSAL**
ユニバーサル
**UNIVERSAL**
**УНИВЕРСАЛЬНЫЙ**
عالمي
**UNIVERSAL**
1849 A Istanbul
1855 A Zonguldak
1855 G Zonguldak
1861 A Fez
1861 G Fez

# U

**UNSICHTBAR**
**НЕВИДИМЫЙ**
غير مرئي
**INVISÍVEL**
**UNSEEN**
无形
**INVISIBLE**
**GÖRÜLMEMIŞ**
**INVISIBLE**
見えざる
1867 A Madrid
1867 E Marseille
1867 I Budapest
1869 A Darmstadt

1869 E Fez
1869 I London
1871 A Frankfurt
1871 E Triest
1871 I Paris
1873 A Shenyang
1873 E Paris
1873 I Frankfurt
1875 A Leipzig
1875 E Offenbach
1875 I Berlin
1875 A Marseille
1875 E Offenbach
1877 A Paris
1877 E Frankfurt
1877 I Dresden
1879 A Shanghai
1879 G Tourcoing
1865 A Osaka
1865 G Milan
1891 A Beijing
1891 G Rotterdam
1894 A Fez
1894 G Leipzig
1897 A Leipzig
1897 G Barcelone
1900 A Potsdam
1900 G Frankfurt
1903 A Barcelone
1903 G Shenzen

# U

**URGENT**
**ACIL**
**URGENTE**
緊急
**DRINGEND**
**СРОЧНЫЙ**
عاجل
**URGENTE**
**URGENT**
緊急
1909 A Phocea
1909 G Istanbul*
1912 A Phocea
1912 G Istanbul*
1915 A Dubai*
1915 G Phocea
1918 A Dubai*
1918 G Phocea
1921 G Istanbul
1927 A Anshan
1927 G Istanbul
1933 A Xuanhua
1939 A Assos
1939 G Leipzig
1945 A Shanghai
1945 G Zurich
1951 A Bern
1957 A Leipzig

1957 G Darmstadt
1960 A Amsterdam
1960 G Copenhagen
1963 A Paris
1963 G Paris
1966 A Paris
1966 G Paris
1969 A Siena

# V

**VERBORGEN**
**СПРЯТАННЫЙ**
مخفي
**OCULTO**
**HIDDEN**
隱藏
**SECRET**
**GIZLI**
**OCULTO**
秘匿
1975 A Felantix
1975 G Felantix
1978 A Felantix
1978 G Felantix
1981 A Felantix
1987 A Ticino

# V

**VERBOTEN**
**ЗАПРЕЩЕННЫЙ**
ممنوع
**PROIBIDO**
**FORBIDDEN**
禁止
**INTERDIT**
**YASAK**
**PROHIBIDO**
禁じ手
1993 A Istanbul
1993 E Paris
1993 I Casablanca
1995 A Beijing
1995 E Fez
1995 I Beijing
1997 A Xuzhou
1997 E Rabat
1997 I Chengdu
1999 A Rabat
1999 E Munich
1999 I Shenyang
2001 A Brighton
2001 E Ubud*
2001 I Brighton
2003 A Lausanne
2003 E Istanbul
2003 I Zurich
2005 A New York
2005 D Zurich
2005 G Townsville*

2005 J Postdam
2008 A New York
2008 D Leipzig
2008 G Brighton
2008 J Lucerne
2011 A Ofenpass
2011 D Quebec
2011 G Beijing
2011 J Paris
2017 A Dubai*
2029 A Leipzig

# V

**VICE VERSA**
**VICE VERSA**
反之亦然
**VICE VERSA**
**TAM TERSI**
**VICEVERSA**
逆もあり
**VICE VERSA**
**НАОБОРОТ**
والعكس
2035 A Zurich
2035 G Paris
2038 A Phocea
2038 G Hamburg
2041 A Potsdam
2041 G Vence
2047 A Prague

# V

**VOILÉ**
**ÖRTÜLÜ**
**VELADO**
秘密のベール
**VERHÜLLT**
**ЗАВУАЛИРОВАННЫЙ**
محجوب
**VELADO**
**VEILED**
遮掩
2053 A Rotterdam
2053 D Rotterdam
2053 G Rotterdam
2053 J Rotterdam
2056 A Rotterdam
2056 D Rotterdam
2056 G Rotterdam
2056 J Rotterdam
2059 A Postdam
2059 D Rotterdam
2059 G Rotterdam
2059 J Rotterdam
2062 A Rotterdam
2062 D Rotterdam
2062 G Rotterdam
2062 J Rotterdam
2065 A Rotterdam

2065 D Rotterdam
2065 G Rotterdam
2065 J Rotterdam

# V

**VULNÉRABLE**
**SAVUNMASIZ**
**VULNERABLE**
脆弱
**VERLETZLICH**
**УЯЗВИМЫЙ**
عرضة للانتقاد
**VULNERAVEL**
**VULNERABLE**
脆弱
2071 A Paris
2077 A Rabat
2083 A Nicosia
2083 G Shenyang
2086 A Barcelone
2086 G Osaka
2089 A Osaka
2089 G Paris
2092 A Fez
2092 G Nicosia
2095 A Nicosia
2095 G Montreal

# W

**WARTEND**
**ОЖИДАЮЩИЙ**
منتظر
**À ESPERA**
**WAITING**
等待
**EN ATTENTE**
**BEKLEYEN**
**ESPERANDO**
待機
2101 A La Habana
2101 G Hannover
2107 A Belediyiesi
2107 G Phocea
2113 A Dailin
2113 G Ubud*

# W

**WAS IST DAS?**
**ЧТО ЭТО?**
ما هذا؟
**O QUE É?**
**WHAT IS IT?**
这是什么？
**QU'EST-CE?**
**BU NEDIR?**
**¿QUÉ ES?**
これは何？
2119 A Paris

# X

**X-MAL**
**Х РАЗ**
× مرات
**N VEZES**
**X-TIMES**
多次
**FRÉQUENT**
**BILINMEYEN ZAMANLAR**
**X VECES**
幾度となく

2125 A Zurich
2125 G Zurich
2131 A Zurich
2131 G Zurich
2127 A Paris
2137 G Paris

# Y

**YELLOW**
黄色
**JAUNE**
**SARI**
**AMARILLO**
黄色
**GELB**
**ЖЕЛТЫЙ**
أصفر
**AMARELO**

2143 A Cadaques
2143 D Leipzig
2143 G Tourcoing
2143 J Montreal
2144 A s'Gravenhage
2144 D Rotterdam
2144 G Mainz
2144 J Barcelone
2146 D Zurich
2146 G Lucerne
2147 A Darmstadt
2147 D Rio de Janeiro
2147 J San Francisco
2149 A Cologne
2149 D Zurich
2149 G Nice
2149 J Leipzig
2150 A Frankfurt
2150 D Bel Horizonte
2150 G Townsville*
2150 J Lyon
2152 A Frankfurt
2152 D Chengdu
2152 G Basel
2152 J Darmsatdt
2153 A Rotterdam
2153 D Townsville*
2153 G Fez
2153 J Lyon
2155 A Townsville*

# Z

**ZEBRA-STRIPED**
斑马纹
**ZÉBRÉ**
**ZEBRA-DESENLI**
**RAYADO**
縞模様
**GESTREIFT**
**ПОЛОСАТЫЙ**
مخطط كالحمار الوحشي
**LISTRADO**

2161 G Berlin
2167 A Frankfurt
2175 A Frankfurt
2175 G Osnabrück

# Z

**ZEITGENÖSSISCH**
**СОВРЕМЕННЫЙ**
معاصر
**CONTEMPORÂNEO**
**CONTEMPORARY**
当代
**CONTEMPORAIN**
**ÇAĞDAŞ**
**CONTEMPORÁNEO**
現代風

2191 A Hannover
2191 G Berlin
2194 A Zurich
2194 G Frankfurt
2197 A Paris
2197 G Rotterdam
2200 A Zurich
2200 G Leipzig
2203 A Interlaken
2203 G Okaukuejo

# Z

**ZWECKLOS**
**БЕСПОЛЕЗНЫЙ**
بلا فائدة
**INÚTIL**
**USELESS**
无用
**INUTILE**
**YARARSIZ**
**INÚTIL**
役立たず

2209 A Nicosia

Ruedi Baur, born in Paris. Designer, professor and head
of the institute of research, "design2context", of the HGK
Zürich. Lives and works in Paris and Zürich.

Isabel Naegele, born in Plainfield/NJ, USA. Physician in
her first life, now designer and professor of design principles
and typography at the Fachhochschule (University of
Applied Sciences) Mainz. Lives in Darmstadt.

We are grateful to Strasbourg's Ecole supérieure des
art décoratifs and La Chaufferie for their substantial
support of the conception and design of this book during
Ruedi Baur's exhibition "U.Eur + CH ou other nationalities"
of 1999. Hence it is with pleasure that we dedicate this
book to those in charge of that joint effort: Jean Pierre
Greff and Philippe Delangle.

Photo Credits
All photos by Ruedi Baur and Isabel Naegele, except those
with an asterisk (*).

With special thanks to Tanja Backe, Gaby Berg, Andreas
Heinecke, Olaf Joksch, Klara Kletzka, Claudia Knör,
Viola Lutz, Christine and Walter Naegele, Ingrid Naegele-
Zimmermann, Ute Schauer, Gerlinde Schuller, Andreas
Spamer, Jean Ulysses Voelker and Günther Stolzenberger
for their support and contributions.

Design: Ruedi Baur, Isabel Naegele
Translation: ManRey Übersetzungen GmbH, CH-Baden
Typography: Integral Lars Müller/Gabriela König
Printing: Vetsch & Co AG, CH-Köniz
Binding: Buchbinderei Schumacher AG, CH-Schmitten

Printed in Switzerland



ISBN 3-03778-012-6

Lars Müller Publishers
5401 Baden/Switzerland
www.lars-muller-publishers.com